THE GREATEST VICTORY

THE GREATEST VICTORY

Canada's One Hundred Days, 1918

J.L. GRANATSTEIN

OXFORD
UNIVERSITY PRESS

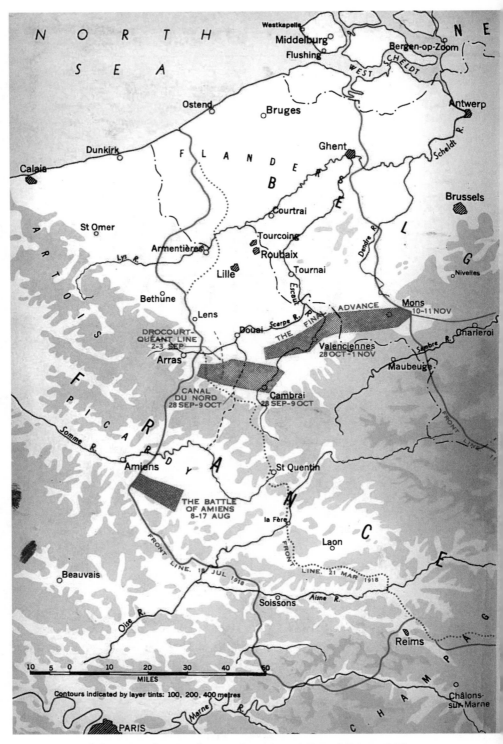

NORTH SEA

Westkapelle
Middelburg
Flushing
Bergen-op-Zoom
NE

WEST SCHELDT

Ostend
Bruges
Antwerp
Scheldt R.

Dunkirk
FLANDERS
Ghent
BE
Calais

St Omer
Courtrai
Tourcoing
Roubaix
Lille
Armentières
Lys R.
L
G
Nivelles
Tournai
Dendre R.

ARTOIS
Bethune
Lens
Douai
Scarpe R.
THE FINAL ADVANCE
Mons
10-11 NOV
Charleroi
Escaut R.

DROCOURT-
QUÉANT LINE
2-3 SEP
Arras
Valenciennes
28 OCT-1 NOV
Sambre R.
Maubeuge

FPICARDY
CANAL
DU NORD
28 SEP-9 OCT
Cambrai
28 SEP-9 OCT
FRONT LINE

Somme R.
Amiens
St Quentin
AN

THE BATTLE
OF AMIENS
8-17 AUG
la Fère
C
E

Beauvais
FRONT LINE 18 JUL 1918
FRONT LINE 21 MAR 1918
Laon

Oise R.
Soissons
Aisne R.
G

10 5 0   10   20   30   40   50
MILES
Reims

Contours indicated by layer tints: 100, 200, 400 metres
P
A
M

Marne R.
PARIS
Châlons-
sur-Marne
CH

From G.W.L. Nicholson, *Canadian Expeditionary Force 1914–19* (Queen's Printer 1962).

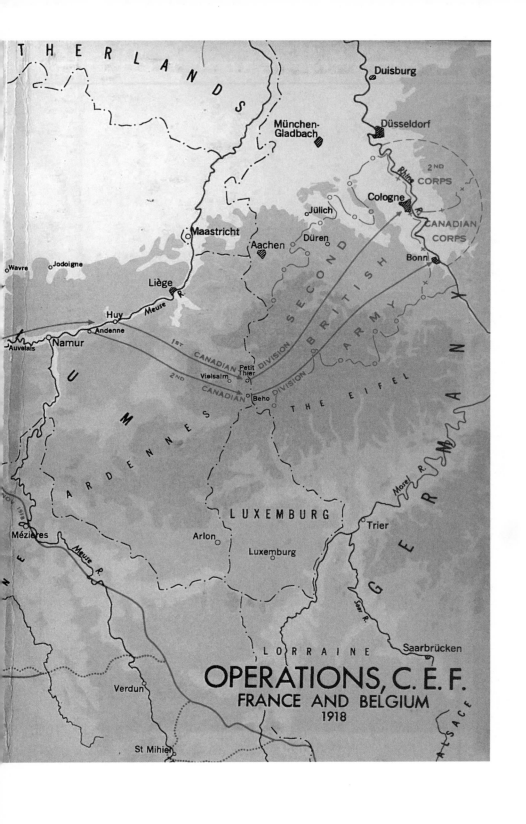

OPERATIONS, C. E. F.
FRANCE AND BELGIUM
1918

For Linda

OXFORD
UNIVERSITY PRESS

Oxford University Press is a department of the University of Oxford.
It furthers the University's objective of excellence in research, scholarship,
and education by publishing worldwide. Oxford is a registered trade mark of
Oxford University Press in the UK and in certain other countries.

Published in Canada by
Oxford University Press
8 Sampson Mews, Suite 204,
Don Mills, Ontario M3C 0H5 Canada

www.oupcanada.com

Library and Archives Canada Cataloguing in Publication

Granatstein, J. L., 1939–, author
The greatest victory : Canada's one hundred days, 1918 / J.L. Granatstein.

Includes bibliographical references and index.
ISBN 978–0–19–900931–2 (bound)

1. Canada. Canadian Army. Canadian Corps—History. 2. Canada. Canadian
Army—History—World War, 1914–1918. 3. World War, 1914–1918—Regimental
histories—Canada. 4. World War, 1914–1918—Campaigns—Western Front. 5. Currie,
Arthur, Sir, 1875–1933. 6. Military art and science—Canada—History—20th century.
7. World War, 1914–1918—Canada. I. Title.

D547.C2G696 2014   940.4'1271   C2014-901238-1

Cover image: Dept National Defence/Library Archives Canada/PA-003286

Printed and bound in the United States of America

1 2 3 4 — 17 16 15 14

CONTENTS

Colour Plates

General Sir Arthur William Currie. Sir William Orpen, oil on canvas, c.1918. Beaverbrook Collection of War Art © Canadian War Museum

Major-General Sir Henry Burstall. Sir William Orpen, oil on canvas, c.1917–18. Beaverbrook Collection of War Art © Canadian War Museum.

Field Marshal Sir Douglas Haig. Sir David Muirhead Bone, ink on paper, 1917. Beaverbrook Collection of War Art © Canadian War Museum.

Canadians Entering Cambrai. Frank Brangwyn, ink on paper, 1919. Beaverbrook Collection of War Art © Canadian War Museum.

German Prisoners. Frederick Varley, oil on canvas, 1918–20. Beaverbrook Collection of War Art © Canadian War Museum.

Avenue Leading to Bourlon Wood. William Rothenstein, chalk and gouache on paper, n.d. Beaverbrook Collection of War Art © Canadian War Museum.

House of Ypres. A.Y. Jackson, oil on canvas, 1917. Beaverbrook Collection of War Art © Canadian War Museum.

Dressing Station in the Field — Arras, 1915. Alfred Bastien, oil on canvas, 1918. Beaverbrook Collection of War Art © Canadian War Museum.

Hun Plane Caught in Searchlights - Arras-Cambrai Road - France - Sept 1918. David M. Carlile, watercolour on paper/card, 1918. Beaverbrook Collection of War Art © Canadian War Museum.

The Cambrai Road. Maurice Cullen, oil on canvas, 1918. Beaverbrook Collection of War Art © Canadian War Museum.

The Return to Mons. Inglis Harry Jodrel Sheldon-Williams, oil on canvas, 1920. Beaverbrook Collection of War Art © Canadian War Museum.

Canadians Passing in Front of the Arc de Triomphe, Paris. Lieutenant Alfred Theodore Joseph Bastien, oil on canvas, 1919. Beaverbrook Collection of War Art © Canadian War Museum.

INTRODUCTION

In the last eighteen months of the Great War of 1914–18, the Canadian Corps became "the shock troops of the British Empire," in soldier-historian Shane Schreiber's apt phrase. The four Canadian divisions, hitting with the power of a small field army, cracked through the heart of the German defenses in France and Belgium, smashed enemy divisions in wholesale, and took the vital ground time after time.

Today, Canadians know little of their Corps' history, except for the victory at Vimy Ridge on Easter Monday of 1917. Vimy was important in giving the Canadian soldiers the confidence that they could do anything. However, the greatest victories of the Canadian Corps took place in the critical period from August 8, 1918, to the Armistice of November 11, universally known as the Hundred Days. In a succession of battles planned and directed by Canadian Lieutenant-General Sir Arthur Currie, the Corps' commander since June 1917, these soldiers played a huge role in the Allied victory over Germany in the First World War. The cost in lives was terrible. But there were measurable gains and decisive results.

The Canadian role in the last months of the First World War was unquestionably Canada's greatest contribution to the Allied victory. In fact, Canada's Hundred Days was the most important Canadian role in battle ever, the only time that this nation's military contribution might truly be called decisive. And yet, scarcely one Canadian in a hundred has heard of the battles of Amiens, the Drocourt-Quéant Line, the Canal du Nord, Cambrai, Valenciennes, and Mons. How could this be?

The reason is simple: the Battle of Vimy Ridge is the one Great War event that any Canadian is likely to know. There, "for the first time, Canadian soldiers fought as one unit," Paul Gessell wrote in the *National Post* on May 22, 2013, "under the command of Canadian officers and employing tactics developed by Canadians. And we won," he went on, "trouncing the Germans where our allies had failed and congratulating ourselves ever since."

This book is not intended to belittle the Canadian achievement at Vimy Ridge. Until 2014, I was the chair of the Advisory Board of the Vimy Foundation, an organization that aims to increase Canadians' understanding of the battle and of the nation's role in the Great War. I have no interest in downgrading the Canadian part in what some consider the most important Allied offensive victory to that point in the war. However, Gessell's story, its content a staple of high school and some university texts, is almost completely wrong. Almost. All that it gets right is that Canadians have congratulated themselves ever since.

The Canadian Corps' four divisions did fight together at Vimy for the first time. But the Corps, initially of two and then three divisions, had been fighting since 1915, building on the efforts of the First Division that had begun in the chlorine gas of Ypres in April 1915. The Corps was commanded in April 1917—as it had been since its creation—not by a Canadian officer but by a British lieutenant-general: first E.A. Alderson and, after 1916, by Sir Julian Byng. The commander of the First Canadian Division was Major-General Arthur Currie. Following a visit to study the French Army's methods at Verdun, Currie prepared a report and delivered lectures that had great influence on the way the Canadian Corps trained and fought. British divisions similarly and simultaneously were transforming the ways they trained and fought. Currie was an excellent officer, Lieutenant-Colonel Dr. Douglas Delaney has written, "and he certainly had an influence at Vimy, but it is a long logical leap to assert that a single divisional commander had more to do with the development and execution of the corps battle plan than the man who actually commanded the entire four-division effort—Lieutenant-General Sir Julian Byng." Academic and popular historians, he added, had created the false impression that "Canadian soldiers with Canadian ideas" were responsible for the victory at Vimy and every battle the corps fought after it.

They weren't. Byng's key staff planners for the Vimy battle were British, a group of officers of extraordinary ability that included three who would rise to field marshal rank and hold the post of Chief of the Imperial General Staff: the gunner Major Alan Brooke, who would lead the British Army to victory in the Second World War; John Dill; and Edmund Ironside. In fact, more than a dozen of the imperial officers who served with the Canadian Expeditionary Force reached the rank of general officer, and Arthur Currie, himself a great organizer and planner of battlefield victories, described the British officers who served on his Corps staff as the "best trained soldiers" he had ever encountered. In addition, seven of nine of the Heavy Artillery Groups that put the Canadians atop Vimy Ridge were from the Royal Artillery, and the supplies, weaponry, and ammunition that the Canadian Corps used largely came from the United Kingdom's vast production.

Moreover, a strong majority of the men in the Canadian Corps at Vimy were British-born recent immigrants to Canada, and there were substantial numbers of Americans and others among the more than one hundred thousand "Canadians" in France. There were thousands of Canadian-born, of course, but fewer than mythology has it, and there was only a tiny number of francophones. Only one infantry battalion, the 22nd, was French-speaking in a 48-battalion Corps.

Most important of all, Vimy did not change the course of the war and did not lead in a straight line to the Allied victory in November 1918. Vimy was part of a major British offensive on the Arras front, and the British Expeditionary Force, commanded by Field Marshal Sir Douglas Haig, made some small gains. The taking of Vimy Ridge in a carefully planned set-piece attack was the highlight of the offensive, to be sure, but Haig and his army commanders had made no plans for exploitation, and there were no massed cavalry divisions waiting in the rear ready to fan out over German-occupied territory to turn the enemy's tactical defeat into a strategic rout. All that happened, important as it was, was that the Germans retreated a few miles eastward into new trench lines in front of the industrial and mining town of Lens, where the Canadians would fight into the summer of 1917. Vimy regrettably did not win the war or even substantially change its course.

But Gessell was correct that Vimy was hugely important for the Canadian Corps and for Canada. It cost 10,602 casualties to take the ridge, and the cemeteries around Vimy are full of the remains of the 3,598 officers and men killed there. The survivors, the men who fought through the German wire and cleared the enemy's trenches, knew they had done something special, and they were cock-a-hoop with their triumph. They had done what neither the French nor, to a lesser extent, the British had been able to do. The victory was won, as one young sergeant put it at the time, oddly omitting Ontario, "by men of Cape Breton, sons of N[ova] S[cotia] and N[ew]B[runswick], F[rench]C[anadian]s & Westerners— all Canucks. Canada may well be proud of the achievement."

The Canadians' special élan, building since Ypres in 1915 and forged in the vicious fighting on the Somme in 1916, now blossomed. The "Byng Boys" were good and they knew it—they believed they could do anything. That renown, won at such high cost, gave the Corps its reputation as a crack formation that lasted through to the end of the war. To the soldiers, no matter from where they came, no matter their origin, no matter how short a time they had lived in Canada, after Vimy they were all Canadians and bloody proud of the shoulder flashes and cap badges that proclaimed their allegiance.

The April 1917 victory at Vimy had much the same effect at home. Canada had arrived on the world stage. It was a British Dominion fighting under British command as part of the British Expeditionary Force. But it was nonetheless truly Canadian, and in the eyes of the public from Charlottetown to Victoria, "our boys" had won the day and brought glory and honour to Canada. Vimy Ridge was the battle that became a symbol of nationhood almost at once, much as Beaumont-Hamel had done in 1916 for Newfoundland, and it has remained so for a century, the proof that Canada counted. The placing of the Canadian national memorial atop the ridge, its soaring towers a landmark of great and solemn beauty, cemented the sense that Vimy was all that mattered in the remembrance of the Great War.

But, as General Sir Arthur Currie—who had wanted the national memorial placed where it would commemorate other, greater battles— knew, there was much more to the Great War than Vimy, much more to add to the Canadian Corps' laurels. The terrific battles of the Hundred Days pushed Germany toward an armistice that amounted to unconditional surrender. In those days from August 8 to November 11, 1918, the Canadian Corps played an extraordinary and outsized role. This book will tell the story of the Greatest Victory.

THE GREATEST
VICTORY

ONE

AMIENS, AUGUST 8, 1918

Born in Barbados, Bertie Cox enlisted in Winnipeg and was in the artillery on the Amiens front on August 8. "For four nights before the 8th we worked from dark to dawn preparing our position," he wrote to friends at home. "It rained quite a lot at this time, and the heavy mud made a good silencer for the traffic on the roads. The battle opened up at 4:20 AM the morning of the 8th of August under a heavy mist which lasted until 10:00 AM. It was the sort of ideal morning for a battle which one seldom sees."

"Every gun shot together," Cox went on, "and the thing was off. I never heard anything like it in my life, neither has anyone else, as it was the biggest show that has ever been staged on the Western Front. Several times I could not hear my own gun fire. . . . After 3 hours, I was practically deaf. We fired our first shot at 4:20 AM at 800 yards and in three hours, the enemy was out of our range (6,500 yards)."

"Within ten minutes of the start," Cox remembered in his extraordinary account, "the tanks, by the hundreds, and the cavalry, by the thousands, were passing our guns. It made an awful pretty picture to see the tanks and cavalry looming up in the mist, over the crest, just about dawn. The field guns began to pass at a gallop too, not to mention the infantry by the hundreds of thousands. By 5 AM, the prisoners began to go by and this procession continued all day. . . . We spent a considerable part of the day checking them over, getting souvenirs. . . . They nearly cleaned us out of cigarettes and emptied our water bottles." It was, declared another soldier, "the best executed and best picked out plan that was ever pulled off."

The great Allied attack of August 8 began with a massive advance of eight miles, spearheaded by the Canadian Corps with the four divisions of the Australian Corps and British and French troops at its side. The war had reached a decisive turning point, later acknowledged by General

Erich von Ludendorff, the quartermaster general and chief strategist of Kaiser Wilhelm's forces, as "the black day of the German Army." The war had been lost, he concluded. Arthur Currie's soldiers, the shock troops of the British Empire, had led the way.

⊹ ⊹ ⊹

The victory at Amiens had not occurred by chance. The Canadian Corps, fortunately holding the line at Vimy, was largely out of the action as the German armies launched their huge series of attacks from March 1918 through July. During this period the Corps had been training. It had also developed the defensive positions that were already at Vimy, digging trenches and dugouts, laying wire, and creating an in-depth defence backed by 72 battery positions with ample stocks of ammunition. Their strong positions were almost alone in the British Expeditionary Force (BEF) in not being attacked in the spring of 1918. Being out of the direct line of the enemy attack did not mean that there were no casualties: some of Currie's men had been rushed into the British line to plug gaps; others died in sporadic shelling or on patrol; and from the beginning of the *Kaiserschlacht*, the Kaiser's Battle, in March, the Corps had sustained some nine thousand men killed, wounded, and missing.

At Lieutenant-General Sir Arthur Currie's direction, in May, June, and July 1918, his division, brigade and battalion commanders, engineers and gunners, ran realistic training exercises with and without troops, testing techniques and educating junior and senior leaders. Individual training began the process, then section, platoon, company, battalion, and brigade exercises followed. The infantry platoon reorganized into two Lewis gun sections and two rifle sections, grouped into two equal half-platoons that could support each other in suppressing an enemy position and attacking it. Sections were to advance in rushes and were dispersed to reduce casualties from machine-gun and artillery fire. Fire and movement was the order of the day.

"It is most important that these schemes should take the form of open or semi-open warfare," the Second Division's training instructions declared, "wherein the unit advances by the aid of its own firepower and without the aid of an artillery barrage. Counterattack schemes will also be practised." Charles Savage, who in 1918 was an officer promoted from the ranks, wrote in his memoir of his service,

> I have always wondered whether our training in open warfare was ordered by someone sufficiently far-seeing to envisage the Amiens, Arras and Cambrai offensives and the fighting on the road to Mons, or whether we were being prepared to meet the Germans after they had triumphantly broken the Allies' line. It was the proper training for either contingency so whoever ordered it was betting on a sure thing. And did we train? Day and night battles all over the place: tanks, airplanes, cavalry, artillery: they were all there. And when we weren't busy looking after platoons in manoeuvres of our own we were acting as umpires in someone else's battle. It was exactly what we needed to shake us out of the habits acquired by years in the trenches; and there seems no reason to doubt but that some small part at least of our success in the fighting during the last three months of the war was due to our training. . . .

Initiative was to be stressed now—blindly following orders was no longer the rule. The senior officers worked in the field behind the lines with their troops and devoured "lessons learned" studies from the British and French armies and from their own Corps, division, and brigade headquarters. In particular, they studied the infiltration tactics that the Germans had used so successfully in their March breakthrough to bypass strongpoints, and the Canadian commanders passed these techniques on to their men.

The units spent some time working with tanks, many more of which were at the front than had been in 1917. They practised working with aircraft. They worked relentlessly on fire and movement, using the two Lewis guns in each platoon to provide cover for the infantry moving forward. They drilled with the new phosphorus bombs, used to create a smokescreen; they mastered the Stokes mortar that could fire bombs or lay smoke; and they trained for gas warfare. The Germans employed phosgene and mustard gas, vile weapons that created huge blisters everywhere they touched, and the soldiers practised marching

Training for defence against gas was key for Canadians, and by 1917, gas masks had been greatly improved. DND/LAC

and fighting in their gas respirators. An officer called this training "an abomination of the flesh. I know of nothing more uncomfortable. One went stumbling about the country, half-stifled and almost blind, with the saliva drooling out of the valve down one's jacket."

Most of the training stressed a new kind of war. Infantryman Ken Foster recalled later that

> It was quite evident now from the tactics we were going through that preparations were under way for another big show in the opposite direction, for . . . we would rehearse day after day. Regular open warfare with tanks and everything. Through the Frenchmen's wheat field we would go, trampling the grain under foot till there was nothing left to harvest. Poor Froggies, their troubles were many. But we had to get on with the war, nothing else but. This business went on till about the middle of July 1918. By that time we were pretty well fed up with attacking hay-stacks and windmills. It all seemed so unnecessary to

us who had been through the same thing too often. On the contrary, it came in very useful when a little later on we came in contact with conditions such as we had been rehearsing, even to the extent of wheat fields, windmills and haystacks.

As the infantry trained, so did the artillery gunners, machine-gunners, signallers, engineers, and the staff. The Canadian Corps had become extremely skilled in counter-battery operations, the task of locating the enemy gun positions and either eliminating them before an attack or neutralizing them during the assault. This required accurate maps and the organization of a Corps Survey Section that made use of an array of technical means, as well as a high degree of coordination with the artillery brigades and well-drilled gunners. At the same time, the gunners worked hard to perfect the creeping barrage, the art of moving the shell bursts forward at the same pace that the infantry could advance. If done to perfection, the barrage forced the Germans to remain under cover until the attackers were on their positions, and if the barrage continued after a successful attack, it impeded the enemy's efforts to retake the lost ground. This minimized casualties for the infantry; so too did firing at a map reference without preregistration of targets and moving the guns forward quickly to provide support. Surprise and mobility were the new words of war.

The Canadians also worked to perfect the use of machine guns for indirect fire, in particular using the two Motor Machine Brigades with their guns and mortars, notably those from the Fifth Canadian Division's batteries attached to the Corps, mounted on armoured cars and trucks. This training was directed by Brigadier-General Raymond Brutinel, a French citizen who had served with the Canadian Expeditionary Force since the beginning of the war. Indirect fire did not aim at a specific target, but instead laid down a curtain of unobserved bullets on, say, a crossroads, ideally denying its use to the enemy who might otherwise have been able to move troops forward. To be effective, this required advance planning and good intelligence on the enemy's movements, acquired by a variety of means—the questioning and searching of prisoners, reports from aircraft overflying German-occupied territory, the interception of wireless communications, and careful reading of captured documents.

The Canadian Motor Machine Gun Brigades made good use of armoured cars, as here at Amiens, to provide heavy machine guns with great mobility. DND/LAC

Currie's headquarters also pressed forward with reorganization. On the battlefield, the engineers played a critical role in getting infantry across rivers and over obstacles. The lesson from trying to function on the muddy terrain of Passchendaele the previous November, digested by the Corps' Commander Royal Engineers, Major-General W.B. Lindsay, and hence by Currie, was that more such troops were vital. The Corps soon had a much-enlarged Engineer Brigade of three battalions and a bridging section in each division, along with specialized units at Corps Headquarters. The engineers no longer would rely on their men supervising work parties of infantrymen. Instead, they would do the work with their own resources. This required a brigade strength of just under 3,200. Currie knew the importance of this arm: "this organization is so necessary that I would prefer to do without infantry than to do without Engineers."

There were many more machine-gunners, too, a centrally commanded machine-gun battalion in each division now consisting of

Currie's engineers became experts at building bridges, sometimes under fire. Without them, the infantry and tanks were bogged down. CWM

three companies with 32 guns each and more men—enough to lug the heavy guns and ammunition around without needing to beg assistance from nearby infantrymen. The British corps, their numbers pinched by casualties and a reduced supply of reinforcements, had cut the number of guns by eight in each division at the same time as their brigades were reducing their strength by one-quarter. Able to draw for reinforcements on units of the Fifth Canadian Division, based in England for largely domestic political reasons, the Canadian Corps was increasing its machine-gun and personnel strength, while the British was decreasing. One estimate—doubtless overstating the disparity—indicated that the Canadians in 1918 had one machine gun for every 13 men, compared with one gun for every 61 men in British divisions. In 1914, a Canadian battalion of some one thousand men had had two machine guns; in 1915, it had four. No one at the beginning of the war had recognized the terrible potential of the machine gun. Now everyone—especially the Canadians—did.

The Lewis gun was the infantry platoon's main weapon. Here, Brigadier-General Victor Odlum (third from left) gives instructions to a machine-gunner while a light tank awaits orders. DND/LAC

Moreover, by mid-1918 the Canadian Corps was by far the largest corps in the British Expeditionary Force. A Canadian division by August 1918 had 50 percent more infantry than a British or Australian division, and Currie's Corps had a hundred more trucks than a British corps, a better maintenance organization to keep heavy equipment functioning, and extra artillery. Currie had decided to keep the disbanded Fifth Division's artillery brigades intact and attached to the Corps, putting more guns at his disposal. In addition, the Corps' general officer commanding the Royal Artillery had the staff to direct the Corps' artillery centrally, unlike the comparable British officer who functioned more as an adviser. There were clear benefits to being a national army, and Currie took full advantage of them.

Sometimes, the Canadians were held back. Currie had wanted more signallers, but Field Marshal Douglas Haig's General Headquarters refused to agree to this. The signallers in the Corps were not increased in numbers, even though their technology had moved forward. New wireless sets were in place at key infantry and artillery headquarters although transmissions could be slowed by the necessity to use codes. Still, for the artillery the new wireless was indispensable, linking division and artillery brigade commanders. Runners, telephones, visual signalling, and pigeons still continued to be used through to the end of the war, a written message remaining the most reliable method of communication.

The staff planners who had spent weeks preparing the 12-inch-thick tactical and administrative orders for the attack on Vimy Ridge in April 1917 now were skilled enough to devise complicated plans in days, and to do so without the paper burden that had previously been necessary. Major Maurice Pope was a staff officer at Fourth Division headquarters, and he noted in September 1918 that Vimy took months of preparation. "Four days ago," he said of the big attack on the Drocourt-Quéant Line, "I knew nothing of this affair and the job is at the very least of equal magnitude." The planners interpreted intelligence reports, and they prepared their plans to fit what they knew and what the Allied high command wanted. General Currie's Corps headquarters drew up the overall attack plan, laying down the tasks for each of the Corps' four divisions. At the division, plans were adjusted to fit each of the brigades, and the brigade staff passed orders to battalions. At the Amiens battle, for example, the 1st Canadian Infantry Brigade's orders covered only two pages. In a matter of hours, Currie's orders could reach Private Bloggs in No. 3 Platoon, C Company, of the "Umpty-umph" Battalion in a simplified form, likely accompanied by air photographs of the objective showing the German position to be seized. The Canadian Corps, its commanders, staff officers, and soldiers alike, were now a highly competent, experienced team. Most of them—except for a few very senior planners—were Canadians, men who had learned their jobs by watching British Army professionals at Corps, division, and brigade headquarters and by going through staff courses. Even the British-born, still half of the Corps' strength, thought of themselves as Canadian through and through.

They had had much to learn. Major Alan Brooke of the Royal Artillery served with the Corps as staff officer to the general officer commanding the artillery. He recalled acidly that

The Commander was a certain Brigadier-General [E.W.B] Morrison. I believe he was a newspaper editor in private life. He was full of bravery and instilled the finest of fighting spirit in the whole of the artillery under his command, but as regards the practical handling of artillery, he knew practically nothing. To start with, I found it difficult to work with him, as I tried to discuss artillery plans with him but found he was entirely unable to take them in. Ultimately, we evolved a process by which I wrote the orders and ensured that a copy of these orders was placed before him. He never discussed a single order during the whole time I was with him. I doubt whether he read them, but am quite certain that he did not understand them even if he did read them.

Brooke, the Chief of the Imperial General Staff in the Second World War, was not simply bragging about his influence and role. The important point, however, is that, properly mentored and trained, the Canadian staff officers and commanders learned their jobs, and soon they believed themselves to be just as good as the British professionals. They were right.

The division, brigade, and battalion commanders also had become skilled professionals, men who had learned their hard trade in battle. The inefficient had been weeded out by Lieutenant-Generals Sir Julian Byng and Sir Arthur Currie; many good men had been killed or wounded; and many had broken down from shell shock, their nerves shattered by gunfire and the terrible strain of making hard decisions that led to their soldiers been killed. The commanding officer of the 27th Battalion, Lieutenant-Colonel Irvine Snider, broke under the strain of fighting at St. Eloi in April 1916, where he had gone for six days and nights without sleep. He had lost 230 of his men there, and he and his officers emerged as "worn, old gaunt men from loss of sleep and horror." Snider was 50 years old—by the end of the war the average age of battalion commanding officers was 37, the youngest being only 25—and he was returned to England suffering from "nervous exhaustion," a casualty of the war.

Men both younger and older than Lieutenant-Colonel Snider cracked under the strain. Some battalion commanders had to be removed because of stress and others because they broke down physically, with stress almost certainly being a contributing factor; another 22 were killed in action or died of wounds. In all, one in eight battalion commanders broke under the pressure of command. So too did brigade commanders, five of whom were moved out of their posts. Some suffered nervous exhaustion that manifested itself in heavy drinking. But the great majority of commanders coped with the stress under which they lived. Those who survived physically and mentally were hard men who could endure the isolation that command forced on them, men who were as brave as necessary, as much an example to their soldiers as any could be. That so many such soldiers emerged from the chaos of battle reveals how war creates the leaders it needs.

That the Canadian Corps could and would fight with great effect was not all General Currie's doing, but much of it was. Very simply, Currie believed his troops would fight hard, and he feared some British troops might not. He noted in his diary on April 11, 1918, during the great German spring offensive, that "many British troops are not fighting well. This is what I expected and what I often claimed during 1917 would be the case. Many of them will not fight and do not fight." Currie rashly expressed this opinion a few days later to British senior officers who "resented any reflections on fighting ability of British Divisions. They do not want the truth they want camouflage and they're getting it. Oh God how they are getting it. . . ." His was too harsh a judgment, made at a time when everyone's nerves were severely strained. But Currie was correct on the key point: he knew that his men could do the job.

Carefully trained and with good leadership and a well-honed organization, Currie's Corps had a new battle doctrine—one that it shared with some other corps in the BEF, but one it had perfected. In their attacks, the Corps of August 1918 bore little resemblance to its predecessors of 1916 or 1917. Success was now measured in thousands of yards, not hundreds. In 1917, doctrine had been designed for a static battlefield. In the summer of 1918, it aimed to practise open warfare. The Canadian Corps' doctrine came about from experience and study—mastering the use of tanks and surprise artillery bombardment, cooperating with supporting aircraft, learning from the Germans' infiltration tactics, and figuring out how to best employ machine guns. In essence, this was the development of a combined arms team. As William Stewart notes, the

Sir Arthur Currie, Canada's greatest soldier. CWM

Corps' doctrine consisted of accurate, intense, surprise artillery fire, quick attacks through enemy "soft spots" by means of infiltration, fire and movement at the platoon level, and support from tanks and the air. The customary preliminary bombardment could be abandoned, replaced by "either a short hurricane bombardment or a total surprise bombardment." There were British divisions and corps that had also enthusiastically adopted combined arms warfare, but as recent research by British scholar Jonathan Boff has found, not all had done so. Currie's Corps was on the leading edge of this revolution in warfare.

At Amiens, the infantry battalions were to attack on a wide front of a thousand yards, double that of 1917. The main body of men were preceded by sections of "skirmishers" (or scouts) who located the enemy strongpoints, then pointed them out to the tanks, which could then target and eliminate them. This would enable the men to filter through the enemy line rather than tackling enemy positions all at once. If resistance could not be evaded, troops were then to employ fire and movement; half the men would rush forward with their Lewis gun firing from the hip, while the light machine gun of the other half of the platoon would provide covering fire along with their rifle grenades. Where necessary, artillery support and tanks could take out serious resistance. Moreover, commanders had orders not to worry about their flanks but to continue the advance, and they were henceforth expected to go forward in attacks, contrary to the earlier doctrine that had commanding officers remaining at their headquarters until the objective had been taken. Speed was the essence of the new doctrine, and the artillery barrage at Amiens moved at a pace of a hundred yards every two minutes and was not preceded by a counter-battery campaign, so as to create surprise. A year earlier in the mud at Passchendaele the barrage had moved that distance in eight minutes—one-quarter the pace—and there was no surprise.

The Canadian commanders had also learned the enemy's counterattack doctrine. They knew, as Ian Brown writes, that after a successful assault, "within twenty-four hours German Reserve Battalions try to get back the position [and] within three days a fresh division is sent against it." To counter this, an increased emphasis was placed on infantries holding their own gains. It was noted by one officer that, "[as] a rule the German, previous to his counter-stroke, endeavours to obliterate our front line. It is obviously advisable not to have our front line where he thinks it is, but in a row of shell holes, connected as far as possible, in front of the captured line."

The Corps' attack doctrine was tested in May 1918 in an exercise that called for a surprise assault using tanks and smoke against defended positions. Brigades and battalions had their assigned objectives, but it was left to commanders to determine how best to reach them. Disseminated to commanders, the critique of the exercise, however, predictably complained that leaders had been too hesitant, too worried about their open flanks, and too wedded to trench warfare doctrine to make the best use of the ground in front of them and their tactical opportunities. Brigadier-General W.A. Griesbach of the 1st Brigade wrote later that "in trenches, everything is cut and dried. In open warfare, everything is wide open." It was difficult to adjust. The most senior officers, those who had done their training before the war, perhaps adapted to the open warfare concept best because fire and movement, platoon rushes, and speedy battalion deployments were similar to what they had learned from the lessons of the South African War. The wartime officers, those who had mastered trench warfare and knew nothing else, had trouble learning the new doctrine. Most infantry reinforcements or replacement junior officers picked up the advanced doctrinal method without difficulty—it was all new to them. But that was in a quiet period with few casualties. In action in the Hundred Days, when losses were heavy, the knowledge level would sink as new—and sometimes badly trained—reinforcements came forward to battalions.

At full strength and well trained as it was at the beginning of August 1918, the Canadian Corps was as ready for its greatest test of the war as it could be. With its four powerful divisions, the Corps had the punch of a small army, and its morale was sky-high. The Canadians believed that they could do anything, that they were unbeatable. With its stress on training and learning, its high degree of coordination, and its emphasis on surprise, firepower, and mobility, the Canadian Corps was ready. At its head was Lieutenant-General Sir Arthur Currie, without question Canada's greatest soldier and one of the Great War's ablest commanders. His sense of the industrial scale of mechanized warfare, his ability to see the battlefield as a system where components at the front and in the rear had to mesh together to create an effective, synergistic whole, and his understanding of how men had to be prepared and supplied to fight had shaped the Canadian Corps into the most efficient, ferocious military organization in the British Expeditionary Force.

✜ ✜ ✜

Able tactician that he was, Arthur Currie was an unlikely military leader. Certainly he did not look the part. Born in 1875 in the hamlet of Napperton outside the southwestern Ontario town of Strathroy, he graduated from high school, briefly attended university in Toronto, and worked as a teacher. A large, pear-shaped man, he carried a big stomach on thin legs. After he moved west to Victoria, British Columbia, in 1894, he joined the local Militia artillery unit. Currie learned the gunner's trade well, and as he rose through the non-commissioned and commissioned ranks in the Militia, he began to play a role as a land speculator in the booming island community. By 1909 he was a lieutenant-colonel commanding the 5th Regiment, Canadian Garrison Artillery, and a married, successful businessman.

As ever, it was boom or bust times in the West, and in 1913 Victoria's land speculators went bust. Currie had overextended himself, his only asset a portfolio of now almost worthless property. But because he had been offered command of the new 50th Regiment, a Scottish-garbed Highland infantry unit, he had access to the $10,800 that had been provided by the government for the 50th's uniforms. Faced with personal bankruptcy and disgrace, Currie siphoned off the uniform money, the equivalent of a quarter of a million dollars in 2014, for his own use. He had a promise from the regiment's honorary colonel to cover the "loan," but the money was never forthcoming, and Currie remained exposed. His embezzlement hung over his head for the next four years until some of his senior overseas commanders paid off his debt. Whether the company that provided the uniforms ever received its money remains unclear.

The outbreak of war in August 1914 saw Currie head off to Valcartier where the Canadian Contingent took form. Garnet Hughes, the son of Militia minister Sam Hughes, was an officer in Currie's Victoria regiment, and his recommendation led Hughes to offer a brigade command to Currie. He accepted and led the 2nd Brigade overseas to England and, in April 1915, into the morass of the Ypres Salient where the Allied position jutted into the German lines (and was thus exposed to fire from three sides). His conduct there during the first major gas attacks of the war and the resulting frantic efforts to hold the line has received both condemnation and praise. Currie left his headquarters and, in some desperation, went to the rear to see if he could find reinforcements for his brigade. He could not persuade British units to come forward to assist his hard-pressed battalions, but he did round up some 300 Canadian stragglers and brought them to the front. His 2nd Brigade did well in the fighting, holding on as long as—or longer than—possible against heavy odds, and Currie merited the praise he received for this; he escaped harsh criticism for going to the rear, an act, to some, that might have seemed close to cowardice. In a battle in which reputations were irretrievably lost or made, Currie had emerged as a cool customer and a comer. When a second Canadian division came to France, now Major-General Currie took command of the First Division.

He led the division through the Mount Sorrel and Somme battles and into 1917. His grasp of battlefield tactics, his good sense, his ability to learn from his and others' mistakes, his openness to ideas, and his willingness to use the firepower of the artillery to save his soldiers' lives drew the attention of Lieutenant-General Sir Julian Byng, who had taken command of the Canadian Corps in mid-1916. Byng sent Currie and a group of officers to study French tactics at Verdun. On his return, Currie recommended that the policy of attacking in waves be ended, that the smaller platoon be the basic manoeuvre unit used in the attack, that platoons and sections be assigned easily recognizable objectives, and that fire and movement be used to take them. Byng agreed, and in the winter of 1917 he implemented the measures Currie had advocated throughout the Corps. At Vimy in April 1917, the Canadian Corps scored a signal victory in part because Currie's suggested changes to tactics and organization had been implemented, and, after Byng was promoted to army command, Lieutenant-General Sir Arthur Currie took over the Canadian Corps.

By this time, however, Sam Hughes and his son had become Currie's implacable enemies. Garnet Hughes had not proved to be a capable field commander, and Currie refused to give him a brigade or, once he had the Corps, a division command. That angered Sam Hughes both while he was a minister and after he was deposed in November 1916. Currie therefore always had to watch over his shoulder, fearing attack both in England, where Garnet had the Fifth Canadian Division on local defence duties, as well as in Ottawa, where the wrathful Sam, still an ever-vocal Member of Parliament, had friends.

But Currie was very capable, so much so that even Hughes' complaints and rants could not dislodge him. He led the Corps to victory at Hill 70 in August, 1917, and he steered it through the hell of Passchendaele. He always undertook his own reconnaissance of the battlefields, and because "he didn't think he was God Almighty," he sought good advice from his subordinate commanders and acted on it. Above all, he cared for his troops' well-being, tried to minimize casualties, and he became a tactical innovator. Currie made his four divisions into an elite formation, widely recognized as one of the very best on the Western Front.

The ordinary privates and corporals at the front, even without knowledge of his pre-war land speculating career, sadly never warmed to Currie. Wilfred Kerr, a signaller in the 11th Battery, Canadian Field Artillery, spoke for many when he wrote that "I thought it a pity that he did not make friends with some privates of the line who could have advised him in advance of the feeling of the rank and file. . . . This would have removed suspicion and sensitiveness and have gained him the confidence of the men," but he "did not seem to have the gift for stroking the fur the right way." Currie was a stickler for discipline, and to many of the men in the ranks he was just another red-tabbed general safely living the good life in a château behind the lines while he wasted their friends in fruitless attacks that, many believed, aimed only to build his reputation.

When the Second Division had to be detached to fight under British command during the German offensive in the spring of 1918, rumours circulated amongst the men that they were being punished by Currie. "Some outfit had looted Arras," believed L.C. Seymour of the 27th Battalion, "and they blamed the 2nd Division for it so, to punish us, they put us in the line for ninety days." This was untrue, and Currie had tried very hard to keep his Corps together, but the myths grew by the day and lived on. He could never become popular with the troops. His written messages directed to the men had a pompous ring to them. He lacked the common touch that Byng had had—the Canadians had been "Byng Boys" but they would never be "Currie's Chums"—and his portly, unsoldierly figure led privates at the front to suggest that there must be no shortage of good food at Corps headquarters.

Those who worked closely with the 43-year-old Currie at his headquarters and in the divisions and brigades admired him greatly, seeing his common sense, his humanity, his devotion to principle, and his desire to lead the Canadian Corps to victory by ensuring that it had the best commanders, training, and equipment to fight and win. No commander, they felt, who beat off Sam and Garnet Hughes as he had done could be anything but a good person. The man who had stolen money before the war, his one great sin in a life of virtue, had redeemed himself tenfold in the eyes of those who worked with him most closely. Oddly, however, Currie did not try to find the money to make good on his theft until late in the war.

Currie was a thinker, a soldier who had studied the almost intractable problems of the Great War battlefield and tried—successfully—to overcome them with innovative methods. He thought and planned for the battlefield as it would exist in the next six months, not only as it was that day. He knew his powerful Canadian Corps would likely be called on to lead the BEF's strategic counterattack, and it was thus no accident that his Corps had practised the tactics of open warfare in the months before August 8, 1918. It was not by chance that the Corps' battle doctrine

Currie studied the battlefield and thought deeply about tactics and weapons. Here, after Amiens, he inspects captured German guns. DND

had been changed in 1918 to emphasize speed, flexibility, and initiative. And it was for the sake of his Corps' ability to fight hard that Currie had resisted British attempts to create a Canadian army of two corps that would increase the rear area "tail" for minimal increase in front-line "teeth." Currie wanted to do nothing that would lessen the opportunity to beat the enemy; he wanted his Corps to build on the high reputation it had already earned, and he wanted the Canadians to be in at the kill.

Getting the Canadian Corps to the Amiens battlefield was not an easy task. In July, Currie's Corps formed part of the British First Army near Arras, and his staff planners were preparing an attack against a feature known as Orange Hill. In fact, this was a ruse, for on July 20 Currie had been secretly advised by Field Marshal Sir Douglas Haig's staff of a planned attack by General Henry Rawlinson's British Fourth Army at Amiens, to the south. The objective was to eliminate the German-held bulge that threatened to cut the vital rail link between Paris and Amiens, and the key to the attack, to be launched by the Canadians and the Australian Corps, was surprise.

Keeping hidden the location of the Canadians, known to the enemy to be shock troops, was vital if surprise was to be achieved. "Wherever the Canadians go," Rawlinson wrote, "they always create suspicion" of a coming attack. "I must publish several lying orders to deceive our own people who do chatter so." The Corps' position could tip off the Germans that an attack was coming at Amiens, and elaborate plans, almost a model for the deception schemes employed in the Second World War, had to be made to cloak the Corps' move to the south.

Two infantry battalions, the 4th Canadian Mounted Rifles and the 27th, along with signals units and two Casualty Clearing Stations, were sent north to Flanders by rail. One officer recounted that "the first intimation [the 4th CMR] had of anything out of the ordinary was when they were suddenly ordered on July twenty-ninth to move . . . and entrain 'for a destination not yet notified.' They were further mystified after entraining to find that they were on what was called a 'Strategic Train,'" a kind of train that certainly none of them had ever heard of before. It was a fast train—which was another novelty—and they passed rapidly through Saint-Pol, Aire, and Hazebrouck and arrived at Arnèke, five miles northwest of Cassel, about seven hours after leaving Acq. "After a good deal of trouble," the account continued,

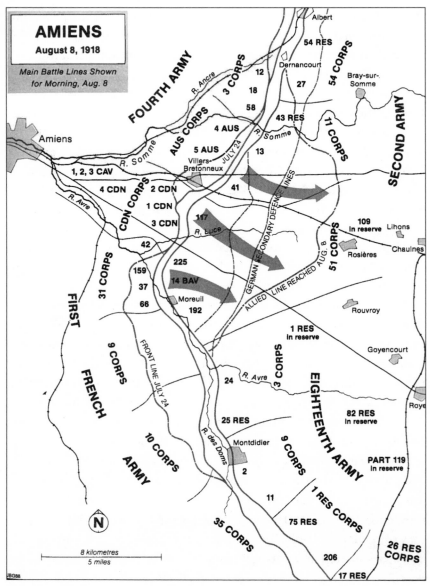

The Amiens battlefield. From Desmond Morton and J.L. Granatstein, *Marching to Armageddon: Canadians and the Great War 1914–19* (Toronto: Lester & Orpen Dennys, 1989), p. 199.

they found shelter of a sort and rested until noon of the next day. Then they marched through Cassel and Steenvoorde to a tented area at St Eloi, near Abeele. On August first they took over part of the line on the La Clytte sector from the Fifteenth Hampshires. The line was nothing more than a series of outposts established during the last German offensive on the Lys, and continuous rain did not improve conditions. One of their most popular Company Commanders was killed by a shell and, all in all, they had a fairly miserable time. On the fourth they moved from the line to Poperinghe and by lorries from there to Nieurlet, near St Omer. There they were loaded into boxcars and passing through Boulogne and Abbeville finally arrived in the Amiens area on August sixth. On the seventh they rejoined their Brigade ready to take part in the great engagement scheduled to start the morning of the eighth.

All this certainly confused the Canadians, as did the deliberately sloppy wireless procedures of the signallers and the ostentatious visits of senior officers who, not knowing they were participating in a ruse, went north to reconnoitre and confer. The planning for the Orange Hill attack meanwhile continued, and only a handful of the most senior staff at Corps Headquarters knew of the coming attack at Amiens. Not until

Heavy artillery weighed tons and, while horses or tractors were usually employed to move them into position, manpower had to be put to work to move 60 pounders—as it was here at Amiens. DND/LAC

July 29, only 24 hours before the Corps began to move south, did the four division headquarters learn of the plan. The logistical challenge they then faced was immense—moving 48 infantry battalions, 646 guns and their ammunition, 162 tanks, and the Corps' array of support units in secrecy and at night to their assault positions by August 7.

German intelligence was not completely gulled by this subterfuge, but it was puzzled, misled by what was happening. To complete the ruse, the Canadian troops were given false information about their objectives, sharply ordered to be silent, and repeatedly warned about spies and loose talk. The following notice was pasted in all men's paybooks and officers' service record books:

KEEP YOUR MOUTH SHUT!

The success of any operation we carry out depends chiefly on surprise.

DO NOT TALK. When you know that your Unit is making preparations for an attack, don't talk about them to men in other Units or to strangers, and keep your mouth shut, especially in public places.

Do not be inquisitive about what other Units are doing; if you hear or see anything, keep it to yourself.

If you hear anyone else talking about operations, stop him at once.

The success of the operations and the lives of your comrades depend upon your SILENCE.

If you ever should have the misfortune to be taken prisoner, don't give the enemy any information beyond your rank and name. In answer to all other questions, you need only say, "I cannot answer."

He cannot compel you to give any other information. He may use threats. He will respect you if your courage, patriotism, and self-control do not fail. Every word you say may cause the death of one of your comrades.

Either after or before you are openly examined, Germans, disguised as British officers or men, will be sent among you or

will await you in the cages or quarters or hospital to which you
are taken.

Germans will be placed where they can overhear what you
say without being seen by you.

DO NOT BE TAKEN IN BY ANY OF THESE TRICKS.

The move of the Canadians from the Arras front to the concentration
area southwest of Amiens by train and bus proceeded much as planned,
although the roads were unfamiliar. Bert Lovell of the 8th Field Ambulance
recalled that "we take a back road, and get lost, at last we come to a sign.
The C.O. attempts to read it with his flashlight some [singing] starts up.
'Lead kindly light amid the encircling gloom. . . . The night is dark and I
am far from home. . . .' As if by magic the dawn comes and we arrive at a
main road and there are our cooks with their field kitchens." Captain Jack
Andrews, a Winnipeg lawyer serving in the 10th Battalion, wrote that his
unit had been on a train all day on August 4. "We arrived [in the Amiens
sector] about 11PM and marched to Lincheux, arriving at 4AM all pretty
well tired out. All movement at night. We knew we were to take part in
an attack in front of Amiens but no one knew when."

Extra air patrols and bad flying weather over the Amiens area kept
the enemy fliers away. Then in the first days of August, the Canadian
units moved at night to their battle assembly areas. Andrews noted that
the 10th had remained at Lincheux for two days "and at 6PM on Aug
6 we took buses to Amiens. Then we marched to Combos wood. The
Batt[alion] were in bivies [bivouac]—tents made of ground sheets—the
woods were full of troops." Meanwhile, artillery ammunition was being
moved to dumps, although the artillery was not permitted to move into
place until 24 to 48 hours before the attack on the 8th. One battery scouted
its position on August 4 and began receiving ammunition the next day—
4,000 rounds in all of explosive and smoke shells. The movement of the
noisy, clanking tanks into position was fortunately covered by cloud that
prevented enemy air observation, but the weather did permit a pair of
Royal Air Force bombers to fly over enemy positions, creating enough
noise to muffle the rattle and growl of treads and motors. General Currie
told Field Marshal Haig on the afternoon of August 7 that "it had been a

hustle to be ready in time, but everything had been got in except 2 long-range guns."

Charles Savage of the 5th Canadian Mounted Rifles, an infantry unit despite its name, wrote an excellent memoir of his war service, and his account rings true:

> The push was to start at four-twenty AM on August eighth, and many thousands of troops, over a hundred tanks, batteries of light artillery, details of engineers, and all the transport necessary to keep this huge force in supplies once the show began, had to be assembled during the hours of darkness immediately preceding the attack. It was a miracle of staff work. To a casual observer, everything would have appeared in hopeless confusion, but such was not the case. Each unit in this huge plan of attack knew exactly where it was to go and what it was to do, and when the zero hour arrived they were all in place and ready. Airplanes hummed overhead to drown the noise of tanks getting into position. Long lines of infantry crawled in single file along the crowded road and finally swung off to right or left to occupy their battle assembly positions. The light artillery took up positions almost in the front line. The roads for ten miles behind the line were solid with troops and transport. When at four-thirty AM the show was started by a hurricane bombardment, each unit in the machine began moving, and this movement forward continued slowly but steadily for eight days.

The Allied attack had the French First Army of seven divisions on the right and Rawlinson's British Fourth Army to its north, this army consisting of the Canadian and Australian Corps and the British 3rd Corps, eight divisions in all committed to the first stages of the assault. Three additional British divisions were in reserve, ready to be thrown into action to exploit success. The attackers had massive gun and tank support and controlled the air with more than 1,800 RAF and French aircraft of all types. Against them, the enemy had only 40 tanks and some 106 serviceable aircraft immediately available. The German lines

The threat of air attack was ever-present. These Canadian trucks all carry recognition panels so that RAF aircraft will not strafe them by mistake. CWM

were held by two armies, but the Second Army had only two "battle fit" divisions while the sector to be attacked by Currie's men was manned by two "average" divisions and part of a third. The defensive system was weak, consisting of unconnected trenches with scattered local wire entanglements. But as always with the Germans, there were heavy machine gun nests in mutually supporting positions between 400 and 600 yards apart, with light machine-gunners in substantial numbers dispersed in front of the nests. Surprise was the critical factor if casualties were to be minimized.

The battle plan relied on the tanks—almost all the new, faster, and more powerful Mark Vs—a hurricane of artillery, and rapid movement of infantry. The Canadians, three divisions forward and a fourth set to go into action later in the day, had the responsibility of striking the main blow on the British Fourth Army's right. The Australians, with two divisions in the assault, were to the Canadians' north, and the British 3rd Corps of three divisions was to the Aussies' left. The objective was to break through the two lines of enemy defences, dubbed the Green and Red lines, from

Tanks were revolutionary weapons designed to cross trenches and go through barbed wire. They were huge beasts, and their scale can be easily judged in this photograph. CWM

three to nine thousand yards east of the start line. The Corps was also to assist the Cavalry Corps in seizing the old outer defences of Amiens, called the Blue Dot line. The Canadians deployed from north to south with the Second, First, and Third Divisions, with the Fourth in reserve. The Third Division faced difficult ground to its front, including the Luce River which could not be forded; and the French attack to its south, due to begin 40 minutes after its own, would leave its flank open. Still, each attacking battalion had from three to six tanks to help overcome the enemy defences, as well as the promise of close air support.

✠ ✠ ✠

The key was the artillery. There was to be a conventional but fast-moving field artillery barrage behind which the infantry were to advance. Heavies were to concentrate on known enemy strongpoints, along with intense fire and gas to neutralize enemy artillery. Harassing fire would hit approaches to the battle area. The Canadian Corps, under its general officer commanding the Royal Artillery, Major-General E.W.B. Morrison, had 17 field artillery brigades, 9 heavy artillery brigades, and 4 siege batteries, or 646 guns. Coordinating the fire of 68 batteries of field artillery was Major Harry Crerar. The counter-battery fire, planned by Lieutenant-Colonel Andrew McNaughton and his staff, gave each gun or group of guns specific tasks to be executed at prescribed times. (Extraordinarily, the two commanders of the First Canadian Army in the Second World War played lead roles in organizing and planning the fire plans at Amiens.) For example, as historian Bill Rawling notes, "one gun could receive orders to fire at target A with 100 rounds over ten minutes, then switch to B with fifty rounds for twenty minutes." Hastily planned but brilliantly implemented, McNaughton's guns suppressed or eliminated the enemy fire, and the advancing infantry captured the remnants of enemy batteries with their guns covered and surrounded by dead bodies and horses.

Artillery was the master of the battlefield, imposing the most casualties on the enemy. Here a gun from the Canadian Corps Heavy Artillery fires east of Arras in September 1918. DND/LAC

Then it all began. The infantry, supported by tanks and the firestorm of artillery, moved forward under the cover of fog and smoke, the surprise complete. At many points, the enemy's forward defences simply disintegrated, and the Canadians, adopting the formations and tactics they had practised since the spring, quickly took their first objectives. The Third Division's engineers, faced with the River Luce and up to 200 yards of boggy ground, built footbridges with great speed while the infantry held off the Germans. But the fog caused as many problems as it solved, some units getting lost, while cooperation between infantry and tanks broke down. "Creeping down the slope like huge great beetles," in Chaplain F.G. Scott's phrase, the tanks, with 36 allocated to the division, nonetheless did good work when they encountered German strongpoints. Lance Corporal Ken Foster of the 2nd Battalion in the 1st Brigade of the First Division, which was at the centre of the advance, said that "the attack was carried out just like any ordinary field manoeuvres, tanks first with us fellows right on their tails. For the first few hours considerable resistance was met with, machine guns were everywhere,

Infantry had the hardest task in battle, advancing to take and hold ground. Here Canadian troops move forward, crouching under fire, with one man, killed or wounded, already down. CWM

but, fortunately for us the Tanks soon put them out of action, provided of course, that an anti-tank shell did not get them first. Without the tanks," Foster added, "I'm afraid it would have been a hopeless task. Certainly there would have been many more casualties."

The 3rd Brigade's 13th Battalion, charged with taking Hangard Wood, ran into a stream that appeared on neither maps nor air photographs, but nevertheless the battalion managed to keep direction. After taking the wood, the battalion met heavy gunfire from an enemy trench "where a large party of Huns held out, using Rifle Grenades and bombs effectively," Major Ian Sinclair wrote. But two trench mortars turned the tables "and assisted in quickly reducing the garrison, who put up white flags."

The advance rolled on. Lieutenant-Colonel George Pearkes' 116th Battalion in the Third Division's 9th Brigade had a difficult time tackling the German trenches, but the previous months' training paid off. "The dash of the men," the battalion history noted, "was most marked, their training in open warfare showing a marvellous difference from the old staid method of following the barrage shoulder to shoulder [with rifles] at the high port." The Second Division's 4th Brigade on the left flank, while losing 588 men, took its objective and captured 17 guns, 71 machine guns, and some thousand POWs. In the centre and on the right, the advancing Canadian brigades similarly made quicker work of the German defenders than expected, killing and capturing thousands. By noon on the 8th, wrote young artillery officer John Scatcherd, "it had developed into the kind of war that I have always dreamt about. Open country with no trenches or barbed wire, and no artillery fire; cavalry dashing all over the place rounding up the parties of Hun and armoured cars rushing about." A scion of the Labatt brewing family, Lieutenant Scratcherd's war did not last very much longer. He was killed on September 3, 1918.

Canadian troops had a reputation for not taking prisoners, something many soldiers had heard about in their training. Private Michael Duggan, who joined the 42nd Battalion in the autumn of 1916, wrote of his spell at a Canadian Base Depot in France that "the most interesting lecture" came from a much decorated British captain "who talked to the men about the German character: 'He had lost one of his own men by the man going out to give some water to a wounded German officer. . . . That is your Germans for you. That is why we British, as well as colonial troops, take so few prisoners. Enough said. The less taken, the less to look after.'"

At Amiens, however, the enemy was surrendering in wholesale lots, far too many to be killed by the advancing Canadians. William Breckenridge was part of a follow-on wave of soldiers that came across a group of prisoners on their knees, begging, "Mercy Kamerad, Mercy Kamerad." Breckenridge grimly remarked, "Mercy Kamerad nothing. You tried hard to get us and now we're going to get you." He had no intention of killing the prisoners, historian Tim Cook writes, despite his harsh words, as he was sharing a grim joke with his fellow infantrymen. At this point his commanding officer came on the scene. The CO coldly appraised the situation and suggested that all the prisoners be killed, since there were too many discarded rifles lying on the battlefield to be safe. Breckenridge was forced to defend the prisoners, admitting that to "kill them in cold blood" would "pay them back at their own game," but also adding that it was "beyond me" to do that. He suggested that they be used as stretcher-bearers. The officer let himself be persuaded, and that was the difference between life and death for these Germans. Sometimes such persuasion would not work. On the other hand, the Germans sometimes pretended to surrender, then reneged and continued fighting. Brigadier-General G.S. Tuxford of the 3rd Brigade noted that on August 8, in one trench his soldiers encountered Germans who waved white flags. "Upon our men advancing they were met with heavy fire again, and the fight recommenced. Two white flags were soon displayed by the HUN, but this time our men took no notice and practically exterminated the garrison." No Canadian then would question this action, but Germans might.

Certainly the Canadian reputation for killing prisoners reached the enemy. At the Canal du Nord in September 1918, Fred Hamilton was captured and, as he made his way back to through the enemy lines, he was beaten by a German colonel and threatened with death. "I don't care for the English, Scotch, French, Australians or Belgians," shouted the colonel, "but damn you Canadians you take no prisoners and you kill our wounded." Hamilton survived, but other Canadians did not,

Surrendering in battle was no simple task. After seeing their comrades killed, soldiers sometimes showed no mercy. But men did give up, often in great numbers, as demonstrated by these German prisoners, taken at Amiens. DND/LAC

the Germans seeing them as vicious elite storm troops deserving the harshest measures. Such treatment only increased Canadian reprisals against their own prisoners when escapees spread word of it.

Most Canadians probably felt some sympathy for their fellow victims of the war on the other side. Watching the parade of captured enemy soldiers pass by his battery, Gunner Bertie Cox noted that "the thing that struck me as being most funny, was, the way the prisoners would dangle right along by themselves, no escort, to the prison cage about a mile away. If there were 30 or 40 together," he added, "they would have an escort, but they mostly passed in twos or threes. . . . They all seem tickled to death to be taken prisoners. They said the attack was a complete surprise." Cavalry officer Ibbitson Leonard, commanding an independent mixed force, watched the prisoners pass by "in hundreds but all well fed looking and in new clothes."

✛ ✛ ✛

Almost on schedule, the next phase of the Amiens offensive began with two brigades crossing the Green line more or less on time, though one was delayed by its long approach march in the swirling fog. Most of the infantry were already beyond the covering fire of the field artillery, so support came from the cumbersome tanks. A demoralized enemy put up little fight, and the Canadians soon were in the German gun lines, wiping out the bulwark of the defences. Only some of the machine-gunners— ordinarily the most stubborn of the Germans—fought to the death, with more than usual numbers surrendering once they were outflanked and under fire. The first Canadians reached the Red line some four hours and thirty minutes after the offensive began.

The attack had thus far been a triumph of surprise and coordination. But as William Stewart observes, while the break-in phase had gone superbly, the breakout phase would stall and exploitation would falter. The tanks, now exposed to enemy fire as the fog lifted in the late morning, were vulnerable, not to mention slow-moving, and supporting aircraft had trouble finding the anti-tank guns, though the smokescreens they put down were very helpful. Some older Mark IV tanks used by the Fourth Division functioned as the first armoured personnel carriers; they carried Lewis gun teams in addition to their own armament, the intent being to get the guns as far forward as the Blue Dot line, the furthest line of the advance, to hold off enemy counterattacks. Nevertheless, German gunners wreaked havoc, firing over open sights and knocking out the tanks in large numbers while the Lewis gunners inside were almost put out of action by the motor fumes if they were not killed by enemy fire.

Unfortunately, the Canadian infantry were not as used to working with tanks as they should have been, especially with the faster and better-armed Mark Vs. Some historians suggest that they had not trained with the new tanks at all; certainly they had not trained long enough to become fully accustomed to working with armour. The result was that the infantry depended too much on the tanks, dropping to the ground at the first shots and waiting for the Mark Vs to eliminate a machine-gun post, instead of taking it out by fire and movement. At the same time, infantry too often ceased their advance if their accompanying tank was knocked out. And the tanks frequently were knocked out quickly or broke down: from 342 Mark Vs on August 8, only 38 survived in running order on August 11. Infantrymen had also learned that tanks attracted enemy fire and were often hit. Private Harold Becker noted that he had passed two burning tanks. "The crews were probably burning to a crisp inside but we could do nothing for them."

The RAF, working closely with the infantry, helped keep the advance moving forward. "Our planes seemed like things possessed," one soldier wrote, and they were "a factor of immense importance in the overwhelming success of the initial attack." The cavalry, meanwhile, held in the rear, could only take advantage of the attackers' momentum if the defenders' spirit was and remained broken. Able as the Army and Corps staff was, it could not react quickly enough to get the cavalry forward to fully exploit the temporary advantage gained by the infantry. As ought to have been realized years earlier, horses were not invulnerable to machine-gun fire, and cavalry unsupported by other arms could not hold the ground they won.

Canadian cavalry, operating in the Third Division's sector north of the Luce River, ran into heavy machine-gun fire that cut down horses and their riders. The Canadian Cavalry Brigade lost 245 men in several "gallant but futile charges." A gunner in the Fourth Division, W.B. Kerr, watched the Royal Canadian Dragoons charge an enemy position at Beaucourt "to our amazement." The "horses went down like nine-pins while some of the men were killed." It was a complete waste, Kerr added. His battery could have routed the Germans with a few shells, "but did not get the instructions and did not see them until the RCD were on their way." One RCD officer who survived reported that "the gunners had a field day for 130 odd men and horses are a great temptation . . . only about 50 all ranks survived—almost every horse was killed." Another soldier in the 49th Battalion wrote of the "unfortunate dumb" horses, "lying around disembowelled, with their entrails oozing out and blood flowing from their broken bodies."

Here as elsewhere, coordination between infantry and cavalry scarcely existed. Brigadier-General Griesbach, the commander of the 1st Brigade, later reported that the cavalry "rode in and out of the area. . . . I am not aware of what their tasks were or what they did." Field Marshal Haig and many other senior officers continued to believe that only cavalry could turn a breakthrough into a great pursuit, but the war had changed completely since 1914, and mounted troops now were simply too vulnerable to heavy machine-gun fire and artillery.

Though the infantry made it to the Blue Dot line by 5:35 p.m. on August 8, exploitation of the advance stalled there; the Germans by now had managed to get enough of their reserves forward—parts of five fresh divisions and almost 300 aircraft had reached the area by the afternoon or evening of August 8—to create a new defensive line, and it was one sufficiently firm to stop any further advance of the cavalry regiments and infantry. One RAF fighter from 5 Squadron, piloted by Captain N. Goudie of Kamloops, British Columbia, forced a hundred enemy troops, massed in a sunken road and threatening to hold up the advance, to surrender by keeping them under constant machine-gun fire. The enemy reserves, moving forward, did not have it all their own way, even though the RAF's effort to seal the battlefield off and to prevent enemy reinforcements reaching it failed.

Thus far, the attack had been a triumph, the usual glitches notwithstanding. Enemy losses were heavy: at least 27,000 killed, wounded, and captured by the Canadian, Australian, and British attackers; Canadian casualties on August 8 were relatively light with 1,036 killed and 2,803 wounded but, unusually for the Great War, with a more than commensurate gain in ground and morale to offset the toll. In one day, the Canadians and Australians had advanced eight miles, twice the distance it had taken four months to achieve on the Somme.

Now, however, the advance began to bog down completely, as the supply organization struggled to move forward ammunition, barbed wire, food, water, and all the equipment needed by the troops. On the 9th, Zero Hour for the 2nd Battalion "was set for one-thirty in the afternoon when the slow and deliberate attack was continued and . . . Heinie had evidently recovered sufficiently to round up some of his Artillery judging by the barrage that greeted us," Lance Corporal Ken Foster wrote. "He sent over a varied assortment of pepper gas, tear gas, poison gas, machine guns, whiz bangs and 'five nines.' And by the careless manner in which those things were falling in our midst, it was quite evident that we were going to spend a very merry afternoon. No sooner had we got nicely under way the boys began to drop, and yet, no matter how many got knocked out there were always the lucky few to carry on to the end."

The First Division was not the only one to face much increased resistance. The Fourth Division had orders to clear the village of Le Quesnel, where it ran into heavy machine-gun and artillery fire. One rather wild estimate put it that on a front of one thousand yards the enemy had 20 to 30 heavy machine guns and 40 to 60 light machine guns. Even if those numbers were exaggerated, in such a concentration, the Germans could not readily be outflanked; fire and movement, the covering fire provided by Lewis guns, were simply not effective. Such an array of firepower, mixed in with artillery fire, could cause terrible casualties, and the German machine-gunners fought ferociously.

But it was the enemy artillery that caused most casualties. Captain Bellenden Hutcheson, the Medical Officer of the 75th Battalion in the Fourth Division, wrote an extraordinary account of this day:

> As we advanced we were frequently under direct observation by enemy balloons directing artillery fire. When one shell landed half a dozen others were pretty sure to land in a very short time within a radius of 50 yards or so of where the first one did, consequently when the first few caused casualties they had to be attended in a shower of debris caused by the explosion of succeeding shells. It was necessary to pass through the streets of Le Quesnel several times during the barrage in order to find the wounded who were scattered throughout the town. I supervised their collection, during lulls in the shelling in a cellar I used as a dressing station. The platoons furnished stretcher bearers. My medical section, consisting of a sergeant, corporal and two privates were with me part of the time, or were in the dressing station when I was out, or they themselves were engaged in looking for wounded.
>
> As the 4th C.M.R. and tanks pushed through the village the shelling again became intense. The Germans were about 240 yds. outside the village. As [we] were attending to some wounded . . . near a street corner that was being heavily shelled, a company of the 4th C.M.R. went by. As the hind of the company reached the street corner about a hundred feet away a shell landed in their midst. About six men went down. As they were going into an attack they could not stop to take care of their wounded. [We] ran to them. The Company Commander lay on his face with the back of his head sheared off. I recall that he had the rank and name of "Captain MacDonald" written on some of his equipment. Three other men were killed and lay beside him. The

Fierce fighting at Le Quesnel in August 1918 left much of the village in ruins. The battle zones in France suffered greatly from shellfire and enemy depredations. DND/LAC

Company Sergeant Major had his leg blown off just above the knee and several men had less severe injuries. We put hurried dressings on the wounded and got them off the corner, which was a very hot spot, into shelter as quickly as possible.

One of the men who had been killed was evidently carrying phosphorous smoke bombs. These set his clothing on fire. We tried to extinguish the fire, but his clothing and body seemed shot through with the phosphorous and it was impossible to put it out. The nature of his wound made it evident that he had been instantly killed and as shells were falling about at a lively rate, we left him. Later in the day when the enemy had been pushed back and things had quieted down I saw his body again. He was almost incinerated.

An American citizen, Hutcheson won the Military Cross for his actions this day. He would later earn the Victoria Cross.

Thomas Dinesen, a Dane in the CEF, also won the Victoria Cross when, on August 12, the 42nd Battalion attacked. Dinesen charged the enemy line alone five times, putting several machine guns out of action and killing twelve enemies with his rifle, bayonet, and grenades. He was instrumental in his unit taking strongly defended positions. In addition to the Victoria Cross, Dinesen (whose sister was Danish author Karen Blixen or Isak Dinesen) was promoted to lieutenant, one of many soldiers who had proven themselves in action to be commissioned from the ranks.

As enemy resistance stiffened appreciably, some of the Canadian artillery was frequently unable to move forward fast enough to continue its customary support. But enough batteries, having trained for this role, did get forward to cover the advancing infantry and armour. This fragmentary diary by Gunner Charles Bottomley suggested the way the events of August 8 and after appeared to one artilleryman:

> **August 8, 1918**—Barrage started about 4:20 a.m. and lasted until 6 a.m. Our lads went over the top and got Fritz on the run. We followed and crossed over no mans land. Saw the dead and wounded. We must have traveled about 8 miles before we pulled into a position at night. I was pretty well tuckered out. . . .

> **August 9, 1918**—Got up at 7 o'clock, had a wash and shaved. After breakfast, our infantry attacked again but was held up in a village. Also around an orchard, the tanks attacked and got the Hun going again. We pulled in the orchard and fired a few rounds. Advanced again and got in action behind a big bush. Fired a few rounds and then stood down. It was great to see the cavalry and horse artillery dashing around.

> **August 10, 1918**—Got up at 6.30 a.m. for a stand [to] fire a few rounds and salvos [to support] the infantry. With the help of the tanks, got the Hun going again. The Canadian Corps were relieved by the 26th Division . . . and they kept Fritz on the run. We were ordered to take a rest for a few hours. Traffic was going forward all day. During the night, Fritz was bombing around the transport and horse lines.

August 11, 1918—Slept under the [gun] limbers. Got up at 7 o'clock. Laid around all day. Fritz was again shoved back during the day. At night, he came round bombing. I dug myself a hole to sleep to protect me from splinters. Had a good nights sleep.

August 12, 1918—Slept in a hole I built to protect myself from the Fritz bombers. . . . Fritz was again bombing our gun during the night.

Another gunner, Bertie Cox, wrote home on August 13 that "it is great fun to have them"—the Germans—"for once on the run." It was not all great fun, however:

On the first day, we had one Officer and one man wounded. The second day . . . one man wounded and on the third, we lost our leader Major Ringwood, while making his reconnaissance for our present position. He's the man we need at the moment. . . . His horse's head was blown off, but he had only one wound, right through the heart. His body was left in a trench over night and the next day, I volunteered with 7 others to bring it in. We looked for hours, before we found it but finally did so, near the front lines. The Hun was strafing us furiously and several times I thought we would need more than one stretcher. We had to carry him two miles and he weighed 225 pounds—no easy job.

To comfort the home folks, Cox added that "the health of the troops, like my own, is in the pink of condition."

After three days of increasingly vicious fighting and a gain of almost fourteen miles, the Canadian and Australian advances had petered out, the Canadian casualties mounting in the fierce fighting to more than 11,700 men for the Amiens operations. Lieutenant-Colonel Ibbotson Leonard, noting that his men had gone without sleep for 48 hours, wrote that he had seen the Australians: "They have done nearly as well as Canadian Corps but each Btn. has to be supplemented by a company of Americans whom the bloodthirsty Australians consider to be more

This evocative photograph shows war as it was in 1918. Horse-drawn wagons pass trucks on a road while overhead a barrage balloon floats serenely. A single German aircraft could quickly turn such a scene into a chaos of death and terror. CWM

bloodthirsty than they are. The Americans are living up to their motto of being over here to kill or be killed, and it is a fine one against such swine as we are fighting."

Currie (joined by Lieutenant-General Sir John Monash, commanding the Australian Corps) now insisted to General Rawlinson at Fourth Army and to Haig that the Canadian effort be halted, maintaining that his Corps faced well-organized defences on the old Somme battlefields and, moreover, had to be prepared to meet a counterattack. If it was to attack again, the Corps must be allowed time for preparation. Perhaps to the Canadian's surprise, Field Marshal Haig and Marshal Ferdinand Foch, the Allies' commander-in-chief, agreed. The advance slowly ground to a halt, and the Canadian Corps soon moved out of the line. At Currie's suggestion, the Canadian Corps prepared to move back to its old stomping grounds under the British First Army near Arras. His idea, promptly endorsed by Haig, was to use the Canadians in another surprise attack, this time against the Drocourt-Quéant (D-Q) Line.

That Currie had enough influence to tell his superiors that the Canadian role at Amiens was at an end suggests both his stature and that of the Corps. The Canadians' reputation as elite and effective troops was fully established, and Haig told Currie on August 22 that the victory at Amiens was "the finest operation of the war." British general and historian J.F.C. Fuller went further and called it one of "the decisive battles of the Western World."

The defeat at Amiens effectively had taken the heart out of the German leaders. Enemy strength had been worn down by the attritional warfare of four years, by the losses of men and equipment incurred in the great German offensives, and by war-weariness at home. The Chief of the General Staff, Field Marshal Paul von Hindenburg understood what had happened when he wrote that "I had no illusions about the political effects of our defeat on August 8th. Our battles from July 15th to August

Commanding the British Expeditionary Force, which included the Canadian Corps, Field Marshal Sir Douglas Haig had reason to thank Canadian troops after Amiens. They had turned the tide of the war. DND/LAC

4th could be regarded, both abroad and at home, as the consequence of an unsuccessful but bold stroke, such as may happen in any war. On the other hand, the failure of August 8th was revealed to all eyes as the consequences of an open weakness. To fail in an attack was a very different matter from being vanquished on the defence." His closest collaborator, Quartermaster General Erich von Ludendorff, called August 8 the "black day," adding in his memoirs that "everything I had feared, and of which I had so often given warning, had here in one place become a reality." There was no hope of resuming the offensive, no chance of winning the war. When Ludendorff reported on the disaster to the kaiser, the emperor interjected that "we have reached the limits of our capacity. The war must be terminated."

The Canadian Corps, the army of volunteers raised by a small British Dominion, had played a disproportionate role in one of the Great War's most important battles.

And there was much more to come.

Returning from the front at Amiens, this tank could move the troops precariously perched atop it or, more usefully, machine-gun enemy gun positions. DND/LAC

CANADA AND THE WAR

Nothing that occurred at Amiens on August 8, 1918, was preordained. Four years of war had created the Canadian Corps; four years of war had changed Canada in myriad ways, and the path forward had been difficult.

Canada went to war on August 4, 1914, for one reason only: because Britain did. As a colony, Canada was bound by the Mother Country's decision, and Ottawa's only right was to determine the scale and scope of the national contribution to the war against Germany and the Austro-Hungarian Empire.

National interests, patriotism, revanchism, and the seductive call of racial superiority—all combined to make war seem almost inevitable once the drums started beating with the murder of the Austrian Archduke Franz Ferdinand and his wife by Bosnian Serb terrorists in Sarajevo. The Austrians pressed the Serbs; the Russians backed Belgrade; and Germany, supported by Vienna, started mobilizing, and soon moved troops both east and west, convinced that a quick war was one it could win. Fearing the fracturing of its empire, Vienna eagerly went along. The British government decided that its long-standing interest in keeping Belgium independent alongside its commitment to support France as a bulwark against an expansionist, aggressive Germany necessitated war. The Russians, already seeing German and Austrian troops mobilizing against them, had to fight, and their French ally had no choice but to support them and to resist a German invasion. Europe and its far-flung colonies were at war. Of the major powers, only the United States, separated by the wide North Atlantic from Europe, remained aloof and neutral.

None of Canada's direct national interests were at stake. The same ocean that protected the United States separated the Dominion from Europe, and so long as Britain ruled the waves, there was no prospect of invasion. Canada was as safe on August 5 as it had been two days earlier. All that mattered to Canadians was that Britain was going to war.

But if legalities drove Canadian involvement, sentiment shaped the contribution. The vast majority of Canadians supported the war with a whole heart, their anti-German attitudes having been forged through the pre-war years by fears over Prussian militarism, growing German naval strength, and the strutting and posturing of Kaiser Wilhelm. Britain was in the right in the eyes of Canadians—right to go to war to stop Berlin's invasion of Belgium, right to assist Paris in resisting the German assault, right to resist the advances of Prussian *Kultur*. Even in French Canada, the usually vigorous anti-imperialist public attitudes were muted, in part because *nationaliste* leader and *Le Devoir* editor Henri Bourassa initially stated his support for the war. He had narrowly escaped internment in Germany where he had been at the beginning of August, but his enthusiasm for Canadian involvement would wane quickly.

Sir Robert Borden's Conservative government quickly offered a contingent for the conflict, and mobilizing it fell to the Minister of Militia and Defence, Colonel Sam Hughes. Hughes was a force to be reckoned with in Cabinet and country, a man of strong passions, raging biases, and immense drive. He loathed professional soldiers, believing them to be barroom loafers and stultified time-servers, almost automatically less capable than highly motivated citizen soldier volunteers. An Orangeman, he disliked Catholics and scorned French Canadians, and all these traits showed up at once as he raised the contingent. By October, considering himself the country's war leader, he had promoted himself to the rank of major-general; in October 1916, he became a British honorary lieutenant-general.

The General Staff in Ottawa, a handful of officers, in 1911 had produced mobilization plans that looked to Militia units to form the basis of any contingent. There were 59,000 men enrolled in the volunteer Militia, but the quality of unit training varied widely. It scarcely mattered, however, for Hughes scrapped the staff's plan, instead sending telegrams to over a hundred regiments authorizing them to send as many volunteers as possible to Valcartier, Quebec, north of Quebec City, where he proposed that his friend and Tory organizer William Price should build a training camp where nothing as yet existed.

Sam Hughes, the Minister of Militia and Defence, was a force, a man of energy and
determination. When he was good, he was very, very good; when he was bad. . . . DND/LAC

In cities and towns across Canada men signed up for service. Why did
they join? Charles Savage, who served with the 5th Canadian Mounted
Rifles, offered his analysis in his war memoir:

> It is always interesting to ask a volunteer why he enlisted.
> Probably the only answer that you will not get is that he did
> it out of patriotism. One seldom hears a soldier use that word.

King and country, the Old Flag, the mighty British Empire are phrases that slip so readily from some people's lips that one is inclined to think that they come from no great depth—certainly not from as far down as the heart. The average man may feel deeply about these matters but he does not like to hear them shouted from the housetop. Generally he despises the shouters: he is embarrassed for them: they make him slightly sick. Some enlisted for adventure, or because they were fed up and wanted a change; while the fear of being thought afraid probably consciously or unconsciously influenced many. I think, however, that the great majority of us enlisted because we felt that—whether we liked it or not—we were committed to a great war, and that other men were being killed doing a job that was as much our duty as theirs. It is all very well to be protected by a regular army, but no able-bodied red-blooded man can sit contentedly at home while his neighbour goes out to do his fighting for him.

The reasons certainly varied but, for many, patriotism, the idea of service to king and Empire, counted greatly in a less jaded era than the twenty-first century. It was a duty to serve, a duty to oppose German militarism and the kaiser's ambitions, and the Dominion of Canada, many believed, could show its maturity by its willingness to contribute to this just cause. For others, the reasons were more personal, as Savage outlined. War was the great adventure, the chance to prove oneself on the battlefield. The war for some was an escape—a way out of a bad marriage or family, or an opportunity to get a (badly) paying job and three meals a day in a time of high unemployment. For the British-born, enlisting offered the opportunity for a free trip "'ome," no small incentive for a working man with limited financial resources. After the war had been going for two or three years, volunteering also put an end to the public pressure and deliberate shaming by recruiters, women, and public and private organizations to enlist. There was some cachet in being a volunteer, none in being labelled a slacker. And after Parliament eventually moved to enact the Military Service Act and put conscription into effect, volunteering let a man choose the Navy or the Air Force or a safe(r) rear area job in the Forestry Corps or Army Service Corps, rather than the infantry. Men soon knew that this was a war without glory, a war of huge casualties and much risk, but few young men ever assume that they will die. It will be the other men, but never himself.

In August 1914, however, the first blush of military enthusiasm was in the air. Enlisting was the opportunity to get overseas, the chance to

Soldiers of the first contingents during their training in Canada, 1914–15. CWM

be among those who would march into Berlin before Christmas, just four months away. This was dreaming even in August 1914, but many Canadians believed it.

A civilian with no military experience, Albert Andrews joined the Fort Garry Horse in Winnipeg on August 28 and left for Valcartier two days later. "We certainly presented a bizarre appearance. Most of the men wore civies [sic] of varying vintage. The officers had everything from kilts to white helmets," he said, but as they marched down Portage Avenue and Main Street to the railway station "with chest out in what we believed the true military manner," the crowds cheered nonetheless. Among those marching down Portage Avenue were raw recruits like Andrews, but also many who claimed to have Militia service. Dr. Richard Holt's detailed study of enlistees, however, shows that more than 80 percent of those who in 1914 claimed to have served had not in fact done so.

Soon the men started arriving at Valcartier, most without equipment, as construction crews hurriedly laid water lines and built rifle and artillery firing ranges, tent camps, and all the paraphernalia of a "modern" military. There would be more than 30,000 volunteers there by early September.

But as Andrews' account and Holt's research suggested, Canada's militia was neither modern, nor well-trained, nor well-equipped, and Colonel Sam Hughes' pushing together of soldiers into newly created, numbered battalions at Valcartier caused only chaos. Lieutenant Alex Thomson of Port Credit, Ontario, wrote that his new 7th Battalion was made up of men from the 10th Royal Grenadiers from Toronto, the 13th Regiment from Hamilton, the 12th York Rangers, the 19th from St.

Created from nothing in what seemed the blink of an eye, Valcartier Camp housed the Canadian Contingent in August and September 1914. It was, most soldiers believed, disorganized chaos. DND/LAC

Catharines, the 34th from Whitby, the 35th from Barrie, the 36th from Peel, and the 44th from Welland, Ontario. Each company in the 7th would have three officers, he said, to be selected "from about ten so some of us are going to get it in the neck. . . . Col Sam Hughes is expected at any time to select the officers." Militia officers frenziedly lobbied the minister for positions, more senior officers jostling for brigade commands. The mercurial Hughes made a captain a major on the spot and put an honorary chaplain in command of a battalion.

Cronyism, Conservative connections, and personal pull largely determined who got what, and the chaos of the camp and the constant juggling of positions and units meant that little real training, other than route marches, took place. "We got to the ranges on the far end of the plain this afternoon, about 4 miles, the ranges have just been put there and there were 1700 targets, " Lieutenant Thomson wrote on August 28, "so you see if we had enough rifles we could soon shoot."

After delay and much confusion, the new units received their Canadian-made Ross rifles, old-fashioned artillery, and newly purchased horses to haul the guns, uniforms, Canadian-designed leather Oliver equipment to carry the soldier's load, and wagons of domestic design. There was one airplane and even shield-shovels, created by Hughes' secretary, to protect a soldier while he sniped and dug. Most of this equipment, including the shield-shovel, failed to work as intended (other than to benefit the government's friends who had the contracts to supply them); almost all of it would be scrapped in Britain or in Flanders.

The First Contingent was a mixture of the untrained and trained. One infantryman, Private William Peden, recalled that the makeup of his unit, the 8th Battalion, was "mostly of men of Old Country extraction, many of whom . . . had seen service with the British Army in India and South Africa, and some with the Royal Navy. The others," he went on, "had no previous military experience, but they had one thing in common, all were young and [seized] . . . the opportunity of visiting their home-land and of seeing again, the parents and relatives they had left behind, when emigrating to Canada."

The Contingent, soon to become the Canadian Division, included 23,211 men born in Britain and only 10,880 Canadian-born—of whom only 1,245 were French-speaking, all astonishing statistics. The British-born immigrants, the most recent arrivals in Canada, felt the call of the blood much more than did native-born Canadians, a generation or more away from Europe. With three centuries in Canada, French Canadians felt this call not at all, neither from England nor France. "It seems a very funny thing," said Private Roy Macfie in a letter to his family in Parry Sound, Ontario, "this is supposed to be a Canadian Contingent, and I think that two thirds of the men that are here are Old Country men."

The tendency of the British-born to enlist in the largest numbers persisted throughout the war, and an extraordinary 228,170 of the 470,000-odd British-born of military age, or 48.5 percent, enlisted. It was not until the end of the war in November 1918 that Canadian-born soldiers made up a majority (51.4 percent) of the 620,000 or so that served in the Canadian Expeditionary Force, a figure that included conscripts. Of 2.82 million eligible Canadian-born males, 318,728 men or 11.3 percent enlisted. More than two-thirds of the 1,811 officers in the First Contingent, however, were Canadian-born, almost all coming from the Militia or the Permanent Force. These men would get most of the senior positions in the Canadian forces at the front throughout the war.

Francophone enlistment is harder to calculate with precision. Serge Durflinger calculates that French Canada supplied approximately 15,000 volunteers during the war. Most came from the Montreal area, though Quebec City, western Quebec, and eastern Ontario provided significant numbers. A precise total is difficult to establish since attestation papers did not require enlistees to indicate their mother tongue, and men who enlisted in one town or city were not necessarily from that place (something that applied across Canada). Though French Canadians comprised nearly 30 percent of the Canadian population, they made up only about 4 percent of Canadian volunteers. Less than 5 percent of Quebec's males of military age served in infantry battalions, compared to 14–15 percent in Western Canada and Ontario. Moreover, at least half of Quebec's recruits were English Canadian and nearly half of all the French-Canadian volunteers came from provinces other than Quebec. It is very likely that at most 50,000 francophones served in uniform, a number that also includes conscripts.

❖ ❖ ❖

In Ottawa, meanwhile, Sir Robert Borden's government tried to organize itself to fight the war. Borden was a long-time Member of Parliament from Nova Scotia, selected to be his party's leader in 1901 because he was disliked less than the other contenders. He had faced countless attempts to dislodge him, but he hung on until he led his forces to victory in 1911, finally driving Sir Wilfrid Laurier's Liberals from office with an anti-American, pro-British campaign. In power, Borden had little evident success, and political insiders suggested with confidence that he would be a one-term prime minister, all but certain to lose in the next campaign in 1915 or 1916. But now there was the war. Everything would change.

The Opposition Liberals had proclaimed a political truce in August 1914, but they kept a close eye on the government's actions. The military was scarcely in their crosshairs, for almost everyone initially praised Sam Hughes for the speed with which the First Contingent had been raised.

Prime Minister Borden cared about the men Canada sent to war, and he visited them in Canada, Britain, and at the front. Here, he watches a live grenade practice in April 1917 at Bramshott Camp in England. DND/LAC

Borden reviewing troops in France, July 1918, while General Currie stands at his side. Borden had great respect for Currie's military talents. DND/LAC

Hughes' military critics, however, would come to the fore in the coming months.

But the rapid-fire purchases that Hughes had made of everything from military equipment to horses and forage drew Opposition attention. Were only Conservative businessmen able to supply the Militia Department's needs? For a time, the Opposition stayed relatively quiet, but they could not turn their eyes away from the mess that Hughes' cronies on the Shell Committee—his personal creation designed to mobilize the small Canadian munitions industry—had made of war production. Other belligerents had their own troubles in getting war production going; Canada's seemed largely attributable to friends of the government, some of whom were given high military rank to go along with the profits they pocketed. The mess did not begin to be cleaned up until 1915, when Borden called on Sir Joseph Flavelle, the "Baron of Bacon," as he was dubbed for his meat-packing businesses, to create and manage the Imperial Munitions Board that soon made Canadian factories hum.

The money to pay the bills for the soldiers and the war contracts— hard to come by in the small government days of 1914, when almost all federal revenue came from the tariff—had to be found by the Minister of Finance, Sir Thomas White. The expectation in August 1914, soon to be dashed, was that the British could finance the costs of the war for Canada with loans. In fact, London would continue to lend Canada the funds to pay for her substantial overseas expenses. But by 1915, the British had advised Ottawa that their money markets could not finance Canada's domestic expenditures any longer, and indeed they urged Ottawa to raise money in Canada, something that the finance minister thought all but impossible.

Instead, in 1915—again at Britain's urging as London scrambled to find the money to pay for its own soaring war expenditures—Ottawa turned for the first time to the slightly raffish Wall Street money markets in New York. This was a historic event, one that passed almost without notice and one that shaped Canada's future. By 1916, 65 percent of Canadian bond issues were being floated in the U.S.

The war was to prove hugely expensive, and White did not believe in raising funds through taxation. In 1916, however, desperate for revenues, he imposed a business profits tax—and in 1917, even more desperate, he followed this with another temporary measure, the nation's first income tax. It would never be repealed, unlike the business profits levy. Necessity also made White see the virtues of borrowing from the public, and in a succession of Victory Loan and Bond drives beginning in November 1915, he raised the bulk of the Dominion's wartime financial requirements, much to his amazement.

A large portion of the money had to be used to pay for Britain's increasing purchases in Canada, purchases for which the battered British Exchequer could no longer find the funds. In April 1917, just as the U.S. entered the war, much to the Allies' relief, London told Ottawa it could no longer afford to pay for its Canadian purchases. In other words, if Canada wanted to sell Britain munitions, grain, cheese, bacon, and everything else, it had also to lend the money to pay for its sales. This was blackmail, plain and simple; Britain recognized that no Canadian government could cut off its sales to the United Kingdom when doing so would outrage patriots, not to mention the farmers, workers, and industrialists whose livelihood depended on the U.K. market. Ottawa quickly caved in, pledging $25 million a month, provided London could find $15 million U.S. for Canada each month to help Ottawa balance its books. The demands of the war had hugely increased imports of steel, coal, and machine parts (among many other things) from south of the border, all necessary to make the munitions and other products Britain needed to fight the war, and Canada had to find American dollars to cover its bills. The problem was that the more Ottawa did to help the U.K., the deeper into the hole it went with the U.S.

The First Contingent of some 32,665 officers and men landed in Plymouth, England, in mid-October 1914 (this number was later adjusted to 36,267 to include all who arrived in Britain by mid-March 1915). The convoy—the largest in history to depart from North America at that time—had carried the men and their equipment in some 32 liners and transports, some crawling with lice, and the escorting ships of the Royal Navy included battleships and cruisers. At Plymouth, unloading the Contingent and its stores took four days because the men, horses, and equipment had been jammed onto the transports without much rationality. The Militia minister had impulsively scrapped the preliminary planning.

From Plymouth, the troops entrained for Salisbury Plain where to their shock they found the good weather of mid-October replaced by unending rain that turned their training and living areas into a sea of mud. Tents flooded, men and horses were miserable and became sick, and very little training could be accomplished. Private Peden complained sadly that "our nice soft Canadian brown shoes quickly took on the appearance of soggy moccasins with turned up toes." The food was no better: canned Argentinian beef or hardtack biscuits that seemed "left over from the South African War or the Riel Rebellion." Trying to ease matters, Britain's War Office billeted many troops in nearby villages which predictably increased drunkenness and cases of venereal disease—1,249 cases of the

The great convoy that carried the Canadian contingent to Britain in October 1914 was the largest ever to cross the Atlantic at that time. Most of the soldiers had emigrated from Britain; most of the officers were Canadian-born. LAC

Training on Salisbury Plain in England put the Canadians into the mud and cold. Sickness was rife, the troops miserable. It would prove to be a foretaste of the trenches in Flanders. DND/LAC

latter were reported before the troops moved to the Continent. "There seems to be about half this contingent bums," grumbled one private in a letter home. "They think of nothing but drinking and getting into all the trouble they can."

By the turn of the year, the Canadians still struggled through the worst autumn and winter in two generations. It rained 89 of the 123 days the Canadian Division, so it now was named, spent at Salisbury. The artillery could not fire their guns until January, the officers knew almost nothing of conditions at the front, and the engineers and signallers were just as green as the infantrymen of the Contingent. But at least the division had its organization sorted out. There were three brigades of infantry, each with four battalions and with four companies per battalion. There were three artillery brigades, each with 16 guns, and the requisite units of field engineers, signallers, and supplies and transport. The division establishment was fixed at 610 officers and 17,263 other ranks. The cavalry regiments and the Royal Canadian Horse Artillery formed the Canadian

Cavalry Brigade, separate from the division. In late February—at last, the soldiers said—the Canadian Division crossed the English Channel to France and became part of the BEF, the British Expeditionary Force.

That the Canadians were deemed ready for action despite their lack of training spoke volumes about the War Office's understanding of the struggle. The war of movement in August and early September 1914 that had characterized the initial German advance into Belgium and France had finally staggered to an exhausted halt by mid-autumn, each side trying to outflank the other and to reach the sea. The war had turned into a war of entrenchments, the lines of trenches soon stretching from the North Sea to the Swiss border. The defensive power of machine guns and artillery made moving out of the trenches all but fatal for infantry.

For two weeks at the end of February, the Canadian Division had its first taste of action when each of its brigades did a seven-day familiarization tour with British units. Officers and men paired off with a peer, manned a small stretch of trench for 24 hours, and the artillery worked with gunners from the Royal Artillery.

On March 3, the Canadians took over 6,400 yards of the front near Armentières, supported a British attack, and suffered their first casualties. By the end of the month, the division had marched north to Ypres, Belgium, the centre of the salient jutting into the German line "like a rounded tumour," as historian Tim Cook put it, "eight miles wide and six miles deep." The Canadians took up their positions between April 14 and 17.

The troops relieved a French division that had left only the most rudimentary trenches full of dead soldiers and human waste, and the Canadian soldiers set out to bring their positions up to "British standards," cleaning and deepening the trenches and stringing barbed wire. They would not get the time they needed to ready themselves fully.

On April 22, the Germans, who had experimented with the use of gas before, found the winds right to use tons of chlorine gas against the French territorial and colonial divisions holding the line next to the Canadians. Completely surprised and unprotected, the colonial troops and the territorial division broke and ran, the men terrified by the effects of the greenish-yellow cloud that had drifted over them. Their faces turning purple, men choked, vomited, gasped, and died. The chlorine

The trenches at Armentières were crudely dug, muddy, and unpleasant. Note that the soldiers wore forage caps—steel helmets did not become generally available until 1916. LAC; drawing courtesy CWM

had not yet hit the Canadian positions, but the division's left flank was almost completely exposed, as was that of the entire British Second Army. The Canadian Division suddenly was all that lay between the Germans and an Allied rout.

Fortunately, the Germans had been unprepared for the extent of their success. The Canadians hurriedly moved platoons, companies, and battalions to their left; British reinforcements began to move forward; and there were still a few scattered bands of the French in their trenches. The rest of the 22nd and all of the 23rd of April saw Canadian counterattacks launched without preparation, much confusion, and heavy casualties as the Germans fought hard to hold their still limited gains. On April 24, they turned their new terror weapon against the Canadian positions, assigning a fresh division and three brigades to follow up the gas attack.

Told to urinate on their handkerchiefs or puttees and to hold them over their noses to (ineffectively) counter the chlorine, the Canadians from the 2nd and 3rd Brigades resisted the enemy, wearing crude respirators, advancing behind the gas cloud as best they could. The Canadian artillery, its gunners also fighting the effects of the gas, fired shrapnel at point-blank range at the Germans. Major John McRae wrote a friend that his battery had fired 3,600 rounds in a 30-hour period, and he observed that his brigade at one point had only seven guns able to fire, two of them "too hot to touch with the unprotected hand."

Complicating the defenders' efforts, their wretched Ross rifles repeatedly jammed in action, and the gasping Canadians had to kick the bolts open. The 7th Battalion's War Diary noted that "at the finish there was no ammunition and almost every rifle bolt had stuck." If they could, soldiers picked up Lee-Enfield rifles from dead British soldiers. Some Canadian battalions, well-led and with artillery support, hung on; others, badly positioned and unable to get supporting fire from their flanks, broke. The 15th Battalion from Toronto suffered 647 casualties in a single day, and its commanding officer was later found drunk well to the rear.

Meanwhile, the 1st Brigade, commanded by Brigadier-General M.S. Mercer and positioned south of the hamlet of St. Julien, faced five German attacks in the afternoon of April 24. Artillery and machine-gun fire slowed down the advancing enemy long enough for a British counterattack finally to halt them, but not before two Ontario battalions were overrun. At the same time, Arthur Currie's 2nd Brigade struggled to hold most of its original front line, but it was hanging on by its fingernails. By going to the rear to seek reinforcements and by bringing

300 survivors from two decimated Canadian battalions forward, Currie helped his battalions. But his Brigade nonetheless had to withdraw on April 25, so severe had been the pounding it suffered.

The Canadians' direct part in the battle at Ypres was effectively over, and the stubborn defenders had saved the situation until enough reinforcements could be brought forward to restore the Allied line. "The Germans thought we Canadians would run because we were not like the English troops," Private Albert Roscoe wrote, "but they found out to their sorrow we did run but the wrong way to their liking."

In their first test, the relatively untrained Canadians had done very well. There were enough old soldiers in the ranks to steady the men against the unimaginable horror of the gas attack, and some commanders had proven themselves. Others were found wanting. But the cost was horrific: more than six thousand in all, including almost 1,300 taken prisoner. Half the division's infantry had been killed, wounded, or captured in a few days, and in fighting in May at Festubert there were another 2,500 killed, wounded, and captured. "I have seen such horrible sights and suffering," Private George Ormsby of the 15th Battalion wrote to his wife in Toronto. "Such devastation and bloodshed you could not imagine it nor believe it unless you saw it." There was plenty of courage in battle but this was no war of glory and chivalry. Nor was it going to be an easy march to Berlin.

Gas was a terrible weapon, and soon soldiers received hastily produced respirators that let them survive a gas attack, though most uncomfortably. The respirators fogged up, frequently filled with vomit that had to be swallowed ("Chew the lumps," sergeants told their men), and interfered with normal breathing. Making matters worse, the synthesizing of new chemical weapons proceeded on both sides; the French soon produced phosgene and both sides made mustard gas which caused dreadful blisters on damp skin, especially in the crotch and armpits, and also affected the bronchial tubes. Soldiers could be and were trained in how to live and fight under gas attacks (though their horses could not be trained, they soon had specially designed respirators), and for some the terror disappeared as such attacks became almost routine. Training, constant alertness, and strict anti-gas discipline were necessities to limit casualties. Under even the best circumstances,

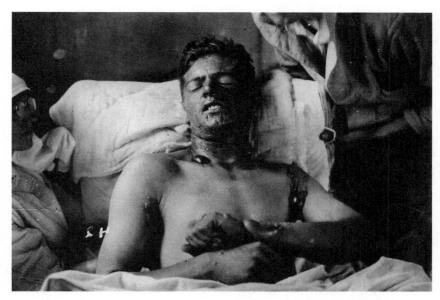

Gas was initially a terrifying weapon of war, and the Germans improved on chlorine gas by developing mustard agents in 1917 that produced pus-filled blisters. DND/LAC

chemical weapons caused great inconvenience; the respirator was claustrophobic and, in hot weather, full protection against mustard gas could cause heat prostration.

The Canadians, among the Great War's first victims of gas warfare, learned the lesson of Ypres well. They would become among the heaviest users of chemical weapons throughout the war, most especially in counter-battery work where gas shells were mixed in with high-explosive rounds, all aimed at stopping the enemy's guns from firing. Certainly General Currie had no qualms about using gas: "we went and carried the battle to the Boche," he told a Toronto audience in 1919. "We tried to make his life miserable. We gassed him on every opportunity and on one occasion ninety per cent of the gas in France was being thrown at the Boche by the Canadians. We never forgot that gas at the second battle of Ypres, and we never let him forget it either. We gassed him on every conceivable occasion, and if we could have killed the whole German army by gas we would gladly have done so."

✦ ✦ ✦

The casualties at Ypres shocked Canadians. No one at home had believed that such a toll was possible. But the impact, while spurring many men to volunteer, led rapidly to quarrels over just which Canadians were failing to do their share. The English-speaking were quick to point their fingers at Québécois, and the very small number of francophones in the First Contingent lent strength to this argument. The Québécois replied that Sam Hughes could have created a French-speaking battalion out of the more than 1,200 men who went to Valcartier. Instead he had broken them up into two different units, and by the time the Division crossed the English Channel there was only a single company of French-speaking soldiers—one-forty-eighth of the Division's infantry.

Another counter-complaint was that the anti-Quebec, anti-Catholic minister had discriminated against the Militia in the province. Desmond Morton notes that in 1870 there were 15 French-speaking units and 70 English-speaking ones across Canada. At the outbreak of war in 1914, there were still only 15 of the French-speaking but 85 English-speaking. In the Permanent Force, moreover, only 27 of 254 officers were francophones, and of staff-trained militiamen, there were only seven. Added to these military factors, French Canadians married earlier than their English-speaking compatriots, had more children, and lived in rural districts that were slow to produce volunteers everywhere. In addition, many suffered medical conditions that resulted from a poor diet. They also had their political complaints about the way the Anglos treated them in Montreal and Quebec City, about the lack of bilingualism in government offices, and about the treatment of French-speaking minorities across Canada, and most especially in the schools of Ontario. These issues rankled, but at root, the French Canadians were *Canadiens* first and only, willing to defend Canada, they said, but far less so to fight for Britain or France in imperial wars of which they knew little or nothing.

What few of the Anglo critics of French Canada admitted even to themselves was that enlistments from English Canada were very light among the Canadian-born. The 1911 Census had shown that there were just over 800,000 British immigrants in the Canadian population of 7.2 million, numbers that were substantially higher by the outbreak of war three years later. The British immigrants were made up in large part of single men with family ties in Britain, but the disparity in enlistments was still striking. Of the 59,144 men enlisted in 1914 and the 158,859 in all of 1915, one careful estimate had it that 63 percent were British immigrants with only 30 percent from the Canadian-born (including francophones). The reality was that, through 1915, most native-born Canadians evidently had little desire to volunteer to fight for king and Empire.

Men were needed. By June 1915 the Canadian Expeditionary Force, as it was now called, numbered just over one hundred thousand in Canada, Britain, and the Continent, and recruitment across the country was in full flight. In October, the government set the ceiling of the Canadian forces at 250,000, and in his 1916 New Year's Day address, Sir Robert Borden unilaterally—and apparently without consulting either his Cabinet or the Army General Staff—raised this to 500,000. "This announcement," he stated, "is made in token of Canada's unflinchable resolve to crown the justice of our cause with victory and with an abiding peace."

The manpower pool was not unlimited. Yet in the nation as a whole, as shown by the 1911 Census, there were 3.859 million men. But as British subjects from 18 to 45 years of age were the only ones officially eligible for service, and some men were essential for industry and agricultural work, the actual number of eligible males was 1.029 million. Then only 820,637 were deemed medically fit for military service (of whom 146,000 were fit only for non-combat service), and the pool was thus much smaller. As the war went on, medical standards relaxed and recent immigrants and foreign volunteers were accepted for service, increasing the pool of males somewhat. Two boys as young as 10 somehow were enlisted, as was one oldster of 78 and one man who was 4 feet tall; the youngest Canadian killed was 14, the oldest 75. Standards for enlistment obviously varied, and judging the medical fitness of potential recruits also depended on the examining doctor. When possible conscripts were examined in late 1917, 24.2 percent were declared unfit for service, presumably a reasonable assessment of the national population's medical state. In Quebec, where most were very unhappy about compulsory service, doctors pronounced some 60 percent medically unfit.

Borden's sacred pledge, for so it became known, ignored the numbers of men available (and willing) to serve, but it may have worked nonetheless as enlistments went very well through the first half of 1916. Many joined up, like Lorne Pierce, a young Methodist minister, because he felt "like a bounder living in safety and ease" while others, like his first cousin, were serving at the front. Many watched the casualty lists swell and remained firm in their conviction to stay out of the army. Nonetheless, by the end of June, there were almost 150,000 men overseas out of the 312,000 who had joined up. Two-thirds of enlistees had been manual labourers, while another 18.5 percent had worked as clerks. Only 6.5 percent had been in agricultural work, and the low numbers of farmers in khaki soon was another grievance for many. Nonetheless, the overall numbers were impressive, particularly so as recruiting was in a mess. The Department of Militia and Defence had authorized individuals and groups to raise 255 battalions to the end of 1916; some succeeded in getting close to a thousand men into uniform but most raised a few hundred and grumpily found themselves combined with one or more similarly raised units. That left disappointed officers and non-commissioned officers. Some units proudly went overseas as the "Umpty-Umpth" Battalion only to be broken up in England, the soldiers dispersed into other battalions from the same geographical area as reinforcements. With more training, the junior officers might be taken on by a unit in France or one readying to go there. However, the commanding officer and company commanders, the lieutenant-colonel and his majors, of the "Umpty-Umpth" were not wanted by CEF battalions in France because they, of course, had no experience of combat. Their choice was simple—revert to lieutenant or remain in England doing nothing. Most chose the latter course, resulting in a pile-up of the disgruntled local notables who had put their lives on hold and their hometown prestige on the line by accepting Hughes' urgings to raise a unit.

In Canada, increasingly strenuous efforts were underway to raise men as the numbers of volunteers dramatically dropped off in the second half of 1916. As early as the spring of 1916, organizations had begun to form to call for conscription as a way to force the "slackers" to fight.

Fingers continued to be pointed at Quebec, where only one francophone battalion—the 22nd Regiment or, as it was known in Quebec, the Van Doos—was continuously in the front line with the Second Division, which had arrived in France in the early autumn of 1915. Recruiting among francophones in Quebec was tepid at best, with almost all the clergy remaining aloof, the local notables reticent—though some did try to recruit with relatively little success. The Chief

Justice of the Quebec Supreme Court, F.-X. Lemieux, blamed reports of drunkenness in the army for slow Quebec recruitment: how could mothers and fathers encourage their sons to enlist when "enlistment appeared fraught with danger for the morals of their sons . . . a school of drunkenness and depravity"?

The reality was that French Canadians as a whole were not very interested in the war. The public pressure in Quebec, such as it was, was to not enlist, and those who did join up tended to be the educated who recognized the seriousness of the situation, the partially assimilated who had attended English-language schools or universities, the adventurous, or the unemployed. By the summer of 1916, 11 French-Canadian battalions had been authorized but recruiting was slow and only five were approaching full strength. Only the 22nd Battalion, the first francophone unit raised, would serve at the front continuously.

There were no hard numbers of enlistments by language, but some tried to find them. Early in 1916, a senior army officer told a Senate

The majority of French Canadians were not emotionally invested in the war, and these officers of the 22nd Battalion, the Van Doos, were atypical in volunteering for service. DND/LAC

committee that 12,000 francophones had enlisted, his educated guess based on the numbers in French-speaking battalions and on French names in other battalions. The French-speaking McNicholls and Scotts would not have been counted while the anglophone Coutures would have been. A Sessional Paper laid before Parliament on June 14, 1917, gave data for the period to April 30 of that year and found that 14,100 French Canadians were serving overseas, a number that included 5,904 recruited outside Quebec. The same source reported that 125,245 English Canadians and 155,095 British subjects born outside Canada were in the army in England and France. More men in all these categories continued training in Canada, but the proportions were unlikely to be very different.

If recruitment in Quebec lacked enthusiasm and had little success, matters were frequently very different in urban English Canada where recruiters often sought out fit men, accosted them, and tried to shame them into enlisting. A letter from one young man to the editor of the *Christian Guardian* provides some indication of the pressures that were built up in English-speaking Canada. "I cannot go to a public meeting, I cannot walk down the street, I cannot go to Sunday School, League or Church, I cannot attend any of the district conventions," he complained. "I cannot even go home and read Youth and Service or the Guardian without being told I am a shirker."

Patriotic women applied their own pressure too. Pierre van Paassen, a naturalized British subject from the neutral Netherlands living in Toronto, recalled being on a streetcar when a woman dressed in mourning showed him pictures of her three sons killed at the front. "Suddenly she began to talk very loudly. 'Why aren't you in khaki? . . . Why do you dare to stand there laughing at my misery? . . . Fight, avenge my boys!', she screamed." Van Paassen left the tram but the woman followed. "A group of businessmen, who had managed to stay five thousand miles away from where the poppies grow . . . gallantly rushed to the woman's aid and forced me to submit as she pinned a white feather through my coat into my flesh: the badge of white-livered cowardice." As Van Paassen wrote, "The following day I enlisted."

As Van Paassen's account suggested, the war involved women intensely. Pat Barker, the superb British novelist whose books focus on the Great War period, wrote on this point, observing that British women had thrown bricks through the windows of "German shopkeepers" and handed out white feathers of their own. "No, it's not true, women aren't more peaceful than men. It pains me to say it," her character Elinor ruminates, "but the one thing this war has shown conclusively is how amazingly and repulsively belligerent women are. Some women."

The war overseas continued, the number of casualties shocking everyone every day. On the Eastern Front, the Russians faced the Germans and Austro-Hungarians, their ill-equipped, ill-led, but brave soldiers yielding ground at a high cost to the invaders. Turkey had joined the German side, and at Gallipoli the Turks inflicted a costly defeat on the Allies; the French and the British—mainly Australians and New Zealanders and a battalion of the Newfoundland Regiment—suffered enormous casualties before a successful evacuation left the Turks in possession of the peninsula. On the Western Front, costly offensive followed even costlier offensive, the toll of killed and wounded mounting inexorably.

The Canadian Corps, initially of two divisions, then three, and by late 1916 four divisions or some 100,000 men strong, had grown in sophistication. Led by a British commander until the summer of 1917, with its senior staff planners almost all being British as well, the Corps was a learning organization with its Canadian officers and men growing into their jobs by understudying the professionals. It now had a full panoply of support services—veterinary units, a range of medical services operating from Regimental Aid Posts all the way to convalescent hospitals in England, salvage units, remount depots, Ordnance parks, and increasing numbers of trucks. Eventually, at its full strength, the Corps' four divisions had 48 battalions or just above 48,000 infantry in all (after the addition of extra numbers to each battalion in 1918), but behind the front there were as many and more men operating the supply and transport system, moving the ammunition and food forward in huge quantities to keep the machine of modern mechanized war going. It couldn't have been more different from the chaos at Valcartier.

And yet, the problems remained. The minister wanted to control the Corps, and his malign influence continued to be felt on appointments

Prime Minister Borden on one of his overseas visits talks with a wounded soldier at a base hospital. DND/LAC

at the front, in England, and in Canada. His friends, given high rank and made his "personal agent" or "official recorder," tossed their weight around and disrupted training and administration in Britain, where Sam Hughes created a council to preside over the mess created there. The council fell apart, only to be replaced by the Acting Sub-Militia Council for Overseas Canadians. That was too much for Borden. Hughes had defied him in setting up his council. The prime minister struck back by establishing the Ministry of Overseas Forces of Canada and appointed the High Commissioner in London, Sir George Perley, as the responsible minister. That largely neutralized Hughes in England. At much the same time, Borden seized control of recruiting in Canada from Sir Sam, as he now was. On November 11, 1916, finally frustrated to the breaking point and increasingly convinced that his Militia minister was insane, Borden demanded his resignation. "The Mad Mullah of Canada has been deposed," one officer wrote. "The Canadian Baron Munchhausen will be to less effect. . . . The greatest soldier since Napoleon has gone to his gassy Elbe [sic], and the greatest block to the successful termination of the war has been removed. Joy. Oh Joy!"

Much of what had remained of Hughes' mystique and power had already been eliminated by the tough and experienced new Canadian Corps commander, Lieutenant-General Sir Julian Byng. The general took command in late May 1916, and it fell to him at once to lead the Corps through the costly reverse at Mount Sorrel, the easternmost point of the

Lieutenant-General Sir Julian Byng, the popular commander of the Canadian Corps, 1916–17. CWM

Ypres salient's projection into the German lines. The Canadian position could see over the German lines, and the enemy was determined to seize this ground. The attack on June 2 fell on the newly arrived Third Division, and a massive artillery barrage blew two of its brigades to pieces, with one battalion, the 4th Canadian Mounted Rifles, suffering 89 percent casualties in what seemed like moments. The Germans also exploded mines just in front of the Canadian trenches and sent six battalions of infantry at the survivors, using flamethrowers to eliminate pockets of resistance. Byng staged counterattacks that had some modest success, the men sent forward in straight lines, carrying at least 60 pounds of kit on their backs. The Germans struck back again, and there were more counterattacks. In the end, the front line scarcely moved, but the toll of dead grew every day.

Byng had developed some respect for the fighting ability of his Canadians, but he realized that he could not abide constant interference from Ottawa. The Minister wanted his son Garnet to have a division command in the field, but Byng had a better man in mind, and he acted, the minister notwithstanding. Appointments to commands in the Canadian Corps would be made on merit, not to satisfy Hughes. The Corps, Byng said privately, was "too good to be led by politicians and dollar magnates." Hughes also insisted that the Ross rifle continue to be used, but Byng knew that the soldiers hated the confounded weapon, and he ordered it replaced by the much more reliable Lee-Enfield. The Canadians' Colt machine guns went too, replaced by Vickers guns, and Canadian battalions received more machine guns, steel helmets, and better grenades and mortars. Byng was an unassuming man, a real professional, and by standing up to ministerial bullying he quickly won the respect of the Canadian Corps. They were the "Byng Boys" now, and their improved discipline, their smartening up, also reflected his influence.

The men of the Canadian Corps had learned their hard new trade. They grew accustomed to the filth of the trenches and to makeshift meals cooked over a low flame, to endless cups of strong tea, and to stale bread in the trenches. They learned how to take care of their feet, applying grease to their toes and changing into dry socks whenever they could to prevent trench foot. But not all the soldiers' time was passed at the front.

Units rotated in and out of the trenches on a regular basis, and even when they were at the front, some parts of a unit's complement were in reserve in support trenches. There they could sleep more and possibly eat better. Further to the rear, soldiers could be billeted in civilian accommodation or in barns, and there they could relax without fear of attack—until enemy aircraft developed the capacity to bomb and strafe well behind the lines. Rest was usually short-lived. An idle soldier was a bad soldier, commanders believed, and men trained, attended courses of instruction, or went on leave if they were lucky. All knew that the time out of the line was merely a respite.

The Canadians' most severe test since Ypres came on the Somme, a long and massive battle that began on July 1, 1916—when the British lost 57,470 men in a single day, including almost the entire Newfoundland Regiment. Fortunately, the Canadian Corps did not become engaged on the Somme until mid-September, but that proved terrible enough. At Courcelette, the Second Division for the first time had the support of tanks, a battlefield innovation, and the artillery fired a creeping barrage

A soldier of the 14th Battalion, First Canadian Division, 1916. CWM

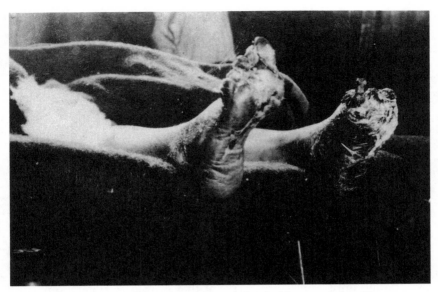

The damp trenches and the unhealthy conditions led to disabling trench foot. Platoon commanders were charged with inspecting soldiers' feet daily and making them use oils to defeat this blight. LAC/DND

Even when dry, the trenches were squalid, claustrophobic. There was little time and little place to rest and eat, and enemy snipers waited for a chance to score a kill. CWM

that let the heavily laden attackers advance in long lines at a walking pace while the guns kept the enemy in their dugouts. But there was not much the artillery could yet do to cut the enemy's barbed wire, and the technology for locating the enemy guns was still under development. The idea that artillery could effectively suppress the enemy's gunfire had still not taken hold.

The 22nd Battalion of the Second Division distinguished itself at Courcelette, clearing the village and driving off 13 counterattacks in 3 days. Of the 22 officers in the battle, 15 were killed or wounded. "If hell is as horrible as what I saw there," the Van Doos' commanding officer, Lieutenant-Colonel T.L. Tremblay, said, "I wouldn't wish it on my worst enemy." Emotional, patriotic, brave, Tremblay had encouraged his men before the attack by reminding them, "This is our first big attack. It must succeed, for the honour of all the French Canadians whom we represent in France." The three Canadian divisions in the attack all performed well, and the Canadians gained 3,000 yards, a huge gain by the standards of 1916, at a cost of 7,320 casualties in one week.

The fight on the Somme continued for six weeks more at British commander Douglas Haig's insistence, attack after attack going forward only to be repulsed or to make small gains of ground. The Canadians' main objective was a German position labelled Regina Trench, a position that the Second and Third Divisions failed to take. The newly arrived Fourth Division finally did the job on November 18, and at last the Corps went into rest. The seven weeks of fighting on the Somme had cost it 24,029 officers and men; British and French casualties were more than 620,000. The Germans were said to have lost 670,000 men.

The Canadian Corps had time to recover, its next major action not taking place until April 1917 at Vimy Ridge. An important feature, the ridge sloped gradually upward, but at its crest it commanded a view to the east and to the rear of the heavily defended German trench lines. The French had attacked it unsuccessfully at a heavy cost in lives, and both sides had dug innumerable tunnels and laid mines in the chalky stone of the ridge. Now it was to be the Canadian Corps' turn as part of a large British offensive on the Arras front.

The Canadians built up their supplies, collected intelligence, and trained carefully for the assault, laying out mock battlefields well behind their lines and running platoons, companies, and battalions through their roles over and over again until the troops, historian Bill Rawling noted, "became somewhat disgruntled with their officers' silly games." Major-General Arthur Currie, commanding the First Division, had studied French attack methods, and his report played a substantial role in reshaping the Corps' organization of its infantry platoons. Platoons were reduced in size from 50 to 35 or 40 men, the intention being that a platoon commander should know his job and be recognized as a leader able to lead his men in action. Each of the four sections in a platoon would have a corporal as leader, while every soldier could take on a specialist role—machine-gunner or bomber—when necessary. The fundamental points were training at the platoon level; flexibility and firepower; fire and movement built around the use of grenades and the man-portable Lewis machine guns; and the maximum use of artillery, all designed to keep the defenders in their bunkers so the attacking troops could reach and neutralize them. And since the Germans always counterattacked quickly, the assaulting troops would need more ammunition, barbed wire, food, water, and supplies of all kinds in order to hold on to the ground they had won.

The soldiers were ready. One private in the Princess Patricia's Canadian Light Infantry wrote to his father three days before the assault on Vimy Ridge that "I am a rifle grenadier and am in the 'first wave.' We have a good bunch of boys to go over with and good artillery support so we are bound to get our objective alright. I understand we are going up against the Prussian Guards."

At the same time as the infantry prepared, the Corps' counter-battery organization greatly improved its expertise. Led by Lieutenant-Colonel Andrew McNaughton, a scientifically minded Militia officer and engineer from Montreal, the Corps' artillery learned how to locate and destroy or suppress enemy guns, which was absolutely critical to the success of every attack. The German gunners were very capable, quick into action, and accurate, using their firepower to assist the defenders in disrupting enemy concentrations and breaking up attacks. But if their guns could be neutralized before the attack, the balance of forces could swing to the offensive and the strength of German counterattacks could be greatly lessened. Using a variety of newly developed and older techniques, including flash spotting, sound ranging, observer balloons, aerial photography, and patrols to nab prisoners for interrogation, the counter-battery staff plotted the location of enemy batteries, working out precisely where they were and how best to silence them. Once the Vimy Ridge battle began on Easter Monday of 1917, these techniques, almost certainly the best developed in the British Expeditionary Force—and Currie's suggestions derived from French tactical methods—proved critical to the Canadian success. The counter-battery staff claimed to have battered 83 percent of the German artillery *before* the attack began.

Byng's plan for the attack had been ready since March 5. His four objectives, each designated by a coloured line on the map, envisaged the taking of the entire ridge and the German second line. The attack was to go in at 5:30 a.m. on April 9, and the carefully staged four-phase assault was intended to conclude with all objectives seized by 1:18 p.m. The Canadians' four divisions had 245 heavy guns and 618 pieces of field artillery in support, one heavy gun for every 20 yards of front and one piece of field artillery for each 10 yards. A new fuse, the No. 106, was used to destroy the enemy's barbed wire, and the infantry

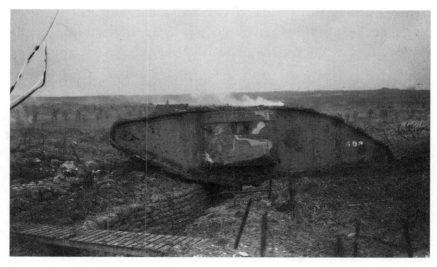

The attack on Vimy Ridge was an infantry and artillery show, but a small number of tanks participated, their terrifying effect on German morale evident. DND/LAC

was to advance behind a rolling barrage that moved forward in hundred-yard increments. It was, wrote Lieutenant Stuart Kirkland, "the most wonderful artillery barrage ever known in the history of the world."

The Germans knew the attack was coming but did not know when, and the Corps achieved tactical surprise by slackening, rather than increasing, its artillery fire just prior to the assault. For the first time, the lethal new gas shells were fired in counter-battery work—the Corps used more gas than other BEF formations—the concentration intended to force the weary German gunners, battered for weeks by a long artillery campaign, to fight wearing their uncomfortable respirators. In the first wave, 15,000 infantry from 21 Canadian battalions went over the top at 5:30 a.m., attacking into snow and sleet, the wind blowing into the enemy lines. The conditions were perfect for the Canadians, and the attack went almost as planned, the First, Second, and Third Divisions taking their objectives, though suffering heavy casualties as enemy machine-gunners and snipers fired at the men. "It was a hell on earth," Arthur Southworth wrote in a letter home, "and I am very lucky to be here today."

Only the Fourth Division on the left of the attack had difficulty in seizing its objective, Hill 145 (so designated by its height in metres), where the defences were especially strong. The Germans, counterattacking repeatedly, held out there until dark, but finally the 85th Battalion from Nova Scotia drove them off. One final feature remained in enemy hands: the Pimple, the northern tip of the ridge. In the teeth of a gale on April 12, the 10th Brigade surprised the Guards Regiment manning

This is a rare, genuine photograph of troops in action, showing Canadians advancing through enemy wire entanglements during the assault on Vimy Ridge. DND/LAC

the position, and by 6 a.m., after hand-to-hand fighting, the Canadians had the entirety of Vimy Ridge and a gain of 4,500 yards. Taking it had cost 10,602 killed, wounded, and captured, a terrible toll, but the victory was a huge gain by the standards of 1917. There might have been a real breakthrough if Haig's headquarters had planned for exploitation of the Easter Monday success, but no one had truly expected victory on such a scale, and no preparations had been put in place.

The soldiers of the Corps believed they had accomplished a great feat, and they had. Honorary Captain William Fingold of the YMCA wrote to his mother that Vimy was "the greatest thing the Canadians have been in yet—wonderful. Of course there have been heavy losses," he went on, "but it was a great victory, and every widow or mother of a man who fell should feel proud and happy the rest of her days that her loved one was willing to give his life in the interest of liberty and democracy—the very thing Christ did." Lieutenant-Colonel Woodman Leonard, a Royal Military College graduate commanding an artillery brigade at Vimy, had written in his diary on Easter Sunday that he "renewed my subscription to London Times for six months." The next day, April 9, he went forward

After taking Vimy, the Canadians set up base camps in the area, sometimes very near the graves of French *poilus* lost in earlier attempts to take the great ridge. DND/LAC

to reconnoitre advanced positions for his guns, was wounded by German artillery fire, and died in a Casualty Clearing Station. But at least the troops could now look to the east from Vimy and see the slag heaps of Lens, hitherto hidden from view.

✤ ✤ ✤

Canadians at home were weary of war. Their gaze focused on the unending casualty lists that appeared with dreadful regularity in the newspapers. Mothers and wives lived in dread of telegrams from Ottawa informing them of the death or wounding of loved ones, and the hothouse atmosphere of war seemed to make every issue more intense. Prohibition became a major issue because alcohol was needed for war production. Votes for women became ever more important, largely because of women's war work and their role as nurses at the front. Corruption mattered more than in peacetime because it was thought utterly unpatriotic to profiteer while men were dying overseas. And the federal election, which ought to have been held no later than 1916, was postponed for at least a year. It would be fought in December 1917.

The overriding issue was conscription of men for overseas service. The pool of British-born immigrants had almost run dry; Canadian-born men, both English- and French-speaking, continued to be reluctant; and the enlistment totals remained low and slow into 1917 while the casualties continued to increase. Sir Robert Borden had been overseas at the time of the Vimy victory and, while delighted at the Canadian triumph, he had been shocked at the casualties. The British, their own manpower barrel thoroughly scraped, pressed Borden to do more. That seemed even more urgent now that the Americans had entered the war in April 1917. It would take many months for the United States to raise, train, equip, and transport its armies to France, and the Germans, having pushed the Russians to the brink of surrender, would surely try to win the war before the Americans' enormous power could be brought to bear. Equally important to some, the United States and its difficult, messianic President Woodrow Wilson could not be permitted to believe that they had won the war. Britain's sacrifices, Canada's losses, made that thought almost unbearable. Borden was very sensitive to this and to the need for men.

Sir Wilfrid Laurier, Leader of the Opposition. LAC

When he returned to Canada in May, Borden had persuaded himself that enough men to sustain the Canadian Corps could only be found through compulsion. He told this to a stunned Sir Wilfrid Laurier and the Opposition benches on the 18th, and Canadian political life was to revolve around the manpower question for the next 18 months.

Borden tried to entice Laurier to form a coalition government with the Conservatives, but the Liberal leader understood correctly that he would lose Quebec to Henri Bourassa and the *nationalistes* if he did. French Canada believed itself betrayed by Borden's conscription bill; if Laurier had joined with the prime minister the sense of betrayal, already exploding into demonstrations, would have been compounded. Laurier therefore stayed out of coalition. Thus, after passing the Military Service Act following a bitter debate, Borden set out on the difficult road to persuade individual Liberals to join with him to enforce compulsory service.

His way was made easier by two important bills that the Conservative government pushed through Parliament. The War Time Elections Act [WTEA] gave the vote to women relatives of soldiers. Women's organizations acclaimed it, but Liberals saw the law as a shameful gerrymander. Their reaction only increased in fury because the WTEA removed the franchise from recent "enemy alien" immigrants. The newly enfranchised women might be expected to vote for Borden and conscription to help support their relatives at the front; the immigrant voters, most brought to Canada by the Laurier Liberals, likely would have supported the Opposition. The Military Voters Act [MVA] compounded the Liberal problem by allowing soldiers to vote for the government or the Opposition, and by allowing those votes to be shifted—by the government side—to wherever they could do the most good. None doubted that the men at the front favoured conscription, but the MVA tilted the balance rather far toward Borden's coalition or, as it was called, Union Government.

Layton Ralston, the Second World War Minister of National Defence then serving as an officer in the 85th Battalion, wrote home to express his—and his soldiers'—point of view: infantrymen simply wanted someone else to take on some of the burden of combat. Conscription had to be imposed to show men at home that they were needed at the front. "I cannot believe that the demonstrations in Quebec represent the sentiments of the people at large," he went on, "but if they do so much the worse for Quebec." The war justified everything in Ralston's and, more importantly, in Borden's view. If Laurier won, the prime minister had convinced himself, Canada's war effort would decrease. Victory over the kaiser, victory to justify the casualties and costs, was essential.

The WTEA and MVA worked on wavering Liberals. The two gerrymandering bills persuaded reluctant provincial Liberals that Laurier had no chance, many jumped ship to support a Conservative-Liberal coalition, and a Union Government led by Borden came into being in October 1917. The subsequent election campaign was especially vicious as Union candidates and propagandists assailed Quebec—was it to be "*Quebec über alles?*"—and Laurier as the kaiser's henchman. The result on December 17 seemed almost preordained. If there was any doubt that Borden would win, it disappeared after the government promised to exempt farmers, busy producing food for the home front and for export to Britain to feed soldiers (and, many said, profiting mightily from this), from conscription. The Liberals swept Quebec, but Borden won English Canada and a substantial majority: 92 percent of the military vote went to the Union Government, enough to switch 14 seats from the Liberals to Borden. The drawback of the vicious campaign and conscription was a pronounced and long-lasting bitterness in French Canada at the election result and at the way their concerns had been crushed by the majority.

Conscription came into effect. The operation of the act was messy, there were bloody riots on the streets of Quebec City, and some 27,000 men fled

The military vote was critical in the December 1917 election, but the secrecy of the ballot in the field was a victim of circumstances. DND/LAC

their homes to escape the call-up, more than 18,000 of them in Quebec. The first draftees had received call-up notices in January, and tribunals, staffed with local notables, heard thousands of appeals for exemption. In Quebec, virtually every francophone called up sought exemption—no surprise to those who had long believed French Canada to be full of slackers. But the same attitude turned out to be true in English-speaking Canada, where almost all—some nine of every ten—sought to avoid military service. Most men nonetheless obeyed their summonses if their exemptions were denied, and trainees began to stream into the camps for their recruit instruction. After the government lifted the blanket exemption for farmers (and all men between the ages of 20 and 22) in April 1918, a reaction to the great German offensive that began in March, even more recruits arrived. Borden had wanted a hundred thousand additional men, and the Military Service Act produced them, the first conscripts arriving overseas in time to be put into front-line battalions by late May 1918. Conscription was a long-lasting political disaster for the Conservative Party, killing it in Quebec and greatly weakening it in rural Canada where the lifting of blanket exemptions for farmers provoked fury; but it did produce the reinforcements the Canadian Corps needed to finish the war.

After Vimy, General Byng received the promotion that was his due and became an army commander. In his place from June 9, 1917, was Lieutenant-General Sir Arthur Currie, the newly promoted and newly knighted general officer commanding the First Canadian Division. The Canadian Corps was to be led by a Canadian for the first time, though Currie wisely insisted on keeping his key British staff planners. Currie was a nationalist, an officer who believed that the Canadians had to stay together because they fought better when all four divisions were in the field under a single Corps command. He was also determined to get his own way, something that became evident in his first battle as Corps commander.

His assigned task was to take the coal and steel centre of Lens, and his orders from Field Marshal Haig and his First Army commander were to seize the town. Currie thought this foolish because his reconnaissance had persuaded him that two hills, Sallaumines and especially Hill 70,

General Sir Arthur William Currie. Sir William Orpen, c.1918. Beaverbrook Collection of War Art © Canadian War Museum.

Sir William Orpen's portrait of General Sir Arthur Currie did not please the Canadian Corps' commander, but it nonetheless captured Currie's intelligence and determination.

Major-General Sir Henry Burstall. Sir William Orpen, c.1917–18. Beaverbrook Collection of War Art © Canadian War Museum.

Major-General Sir Henry Burstall, a regular force gunner, successfully commanded the 2nd Canadian DIvision. Like other Canadian senior offiers, his portrait was painted by William Orpen.

Field Marshal Sir Douglas Haig.
Sir David Muirhead Bone, 1917.
Beaverbrook Collection of War Art ©
Canadian War Museum.

Field Marshal Sir Douglas Haig, commander
of the British Expeditionary Force, as sketched
by British artist Sir David Muirhead Bone.

Canadians Entering Cambrai. Frank Brangwyn, 1919. Beaverbrook Collection of War Art ©
Canadian War Museum.

British artist Sir Frank Brangwyn's lithograph of Canadian troops moving through the ruins of Cambrai in October 1918
limned the emotions of the last weeks of the war.

German Prisoners. Frederick Varley, 1918–20. Beaverbrook Collection of War Art © Canadian War Museum.

Fred Varley was one of the Group of Seven artists whose war experiences shaped his later work. These German prisoners are moving through a blasted landscape looking not unlike a fire-ravaged northern Canadian scene.

Avenue Leading to Bourlon Wood. William Rothenstein, n.d. Beaverbrook Collection of War Art © Canadian War Museum.

Bourlon Wood was a key objective on the route to Cambrai during the Hundred Days. The road to the wood was painted by British artist Sir William Rothenstein.

Houses of Ypres. A.Y. Jackson, c.1917. Beaverbrook Collection of War Art © Canadian War Museum.

France and Belgium were devastated by the fighting, no place more than the medieval city of Ypres, here painted by A.Y. Jackson.

Dressing Station in the Field — Arras, 1915. Alfred Bastien, 1918. Beaverbrook Collection of War Art © Canadian War Museum.

Belgian artist Alfred Bastien worked for the Canadian War Memorials Fund and painted Canadians in action. Here he showed a field dressing station operating on a blasted plain.

Hun Plane Caught in Searchlights - Arras-Cambrai Road - France - Sept 1918. David M. Carlile, 1918. Beaverbrook Collection of War Art © Canadian War Museum.

Soldier artists sometimes found time to sketch in the field. This striking and naïve September 1918 watercolour by Private David Carlile vividly portrayed an incident just behind the front as troops, vehicles, and guns move and fire.

The Cambrai Road. Maurice Cullen, 1918. Beaverbrook Collection of War Art © Canadian War Museum.

Maurice Cullen served as a war artist though he was 52 years old in 1918. His stunning image captured the beauty inherent in even a destroyed landscape.

The Return to Mons.
Inglis Harry Jodrel
Sheldon-Williams, 1920.
Beaverbrook Collection
of War Art © Canadian
War Museum.

British painter Inglis Sheldon-
Williams was named a
Canadian war artist in
1917. His huge canvas of
the Canadians in Mons in
November 1918 succeeded in
grasping "a noble epic."

Canadians Passing in Front of the Arc de Triomphe, Paris. Lieutenant Alfred Theodore Joseph Bastien, 1919. Beaverbrook Collection of War Art © Canadian War Museum.

Canadian troops, painted here in grand style by Alfred Bastien, participated in the great victory parade in Paris.

dominated the city. If he held the hills and if his men could dig in quickly and be adequately resupplied with barbed wire and ammunition, the Germans would be forced to counterattack, as their doctrine demanded. Then his artillery and machine guns could smash them on a killing ground of his own making. His arguments persuaded his superiors that he was right, something of a rarity in a hierarchical British Army system dominated by professional soldiers who ordinarily might dismiss a colonial Militia officer's ideas—no matter how successful he had been in the past. Currie was not a regular officer, and he was much more willing to speak out, even though Douglas Haig found him more than slightly tiresome: "the Canadians always open their mouths very wide!" he grumbled in July 1917 after Currie had badgered him for more artillery support at Lens.

Currie's Corps set out on August 15, 1917, to seize Hill 70, itself strongly defended. The battle was terrible, the fighting intense on slag heaps and in houses. But Currie's planning paid off, and his artillery smashed repeated counterattacks as the Canadians fought for ten days to take and hold Hill 70. "Our gunners, machine-gunners and infantry," Currie said, "never had such targets." The Canadians eventually prevailed, but at a cost of 9,198 casualties. The Germans had broken five of their divisions in the vain effort to defend Lens, and Currie had his first victory on his own.

After some fruitless, costly fighting to capture Lens itself, Currie's Corps had a respite until the autumn. In October it was ordered into the hell of Passchendaele. After the failure of his efforts to break out to Belgium's North Sea coast, Haig's overall strategy had become one of attrition, an effort to wear down the Germans that involved the sacrifice of much of his own manpower. Passchendaele in the Ypres salient became the locus of his offensive from the end of July into November, and many British and Australian divisions had been decimated there. Now it was the Canadians' turn.

The Passchendaele battlefield was a morass of mud, deep enough, viscous enough, that men could and did drown in shell holes. The ground was low and wet, enemy positions overlooking the battlefield from their concrete blockhouses, and the terrain was littered with the dead, maimed horses, and ruined equipment. "The wastage," an infantry lieutenant said in a letter to his father, "was frightful and the ground strewn with everything which moves into a battle area." Currie undertook his own reconnaissance, as was his usual practice, and so dreadful was the battle space that he initially refused to send his Corps there, and certainly not if it had to serve under Sir Hubert Gough of the Fifth Army, a commander Currie believed to be incompetent. His offensive floundering in the mud, Haig agreed to switch the Corps to Sir Herbert Plumer's Second Army, but Currie continued to protest. Finally, he reluctantly agreed to commit his Corps, but not before securing Haig's agreement that he would have all the time he needed for preparation and rehearsals and not before predicting that the attack would cost 16,000 casualties.

Currie was dead right. The battle at Passchendaele, as one private in the 50th Battalion put it later, "was without doubt one of the Muddy-est, Bloody-est, of the whole war." After first taking pains to get his artillery on the firmest possible footing and after constructing corduroy roads so men and supplies could move forward through the mud, Currie began his assault on October 26. The positions captured that day by Currie's troops, Haig wrote in his diary, "are of the greatest importance." They weren't; no position at Passchendaele was of great importance. The first three-day advance, begun under heavy German fire that inflicted terrible casualties, moved the line forward, but short of the intended 1,200 yards. The second phase, begun on October 30 in the cold and mud, pushed the advance ahead another thousand yards. Finally, on November 6, the Canadians staged a quick attack, and the First Canadian Division's 3rd Brigade took Passchendaele—now just a ruined dot on the map—in three hours despite the enemy's heavy artillery fire. "A very important success," Haig crowed. It was a meaningless victory, but meaningless or not, it was a battle won by a highly professional military machine that had learned how to adapt and to fight.

Still, the casualties overall were almost exactly as Currie had estimated, all for a position of no real significance and one that the Germans would take back with ease in their March 1918 offensive. In London in June 1918, Sir Robert Borden told British Prime Minister David Lloyd George that "if there is ever a repetition of Passchendaele, not a Canadian soldier will leave the shore of Canada so long as the Canadian people entrust the Government of my country to my hands." It was a pity he had waited so long to utter that threat.

The Passchendaele battlefield was a swampy charnel house, a horror of mud into which men and machines disappeared. Engineers, here lugging trench mats, were critical. In the rear, prisoners and wounded are just visible. DND/LAC

The Canadian Corps, its reputation as an elite formation firmly established by its role at Vimy, Lens, and Passchendaele, was to be out of action as a corps for the next nine months.

The great enemy offensives that began in March 1918, after Russia had been forced out of the war, fortuitously avoided the areas where the Corps was based. The enemy attacks, labelled the *Kaiserschlacht* or Kaiser's Battle, first struck Gough's Fifth Army and sent it reeling backwards. Then the Germans attacked in Flanders in April and to the south at Champagne in May and July. The Allied lines, reinforced with substantial numbers of newly arrived American divisions, buckled badly but ultimately held. Now short of men (the losses in the attacks had come to more than a million of the enemy's best soldiers) and running low on supplies, the Germans had made their last throw of the dice. Marshal Ferdinand Foch, installed as Allied Generalissimo in the midst of the German attacks, at last was able to begin to consider counter-blows, and he apparently believed the Canadian Corps had to be prominent in any such offensive.

General Currie, meanwhile, had made two critical decisions. Early in 1918 the British had suggested the Canadians form an army of two corps, using the Fifth Division that was stationed in England, and battalions that would be found by reducing the divisional complement from twelve to nine battalions. The British and Australians had already been forced to reduce their division strength because of a shortage of reinforcements. This suggestion would have resulted in Currie's promotion from lieutenant-general to general, the rank of an army commander.

Currie flatly refused, and he persuaded the Minister of the Overseas Military Forces in London to agree. The Corps fought well as a corps, Currie maintained, and there were not enough trained Canadian staff officers to run an army headquarters, another corps headquarters, two additional division headquarters, and six more brigade headquarters; if enough Canadians could not be found, British officers would be required, something contrary to the government and Corps policy of Canadianization whenever and wherever possible. Nor were there enough troops to man the rear-area logistical and support units an army required. Again, British troops would be required. Currie argued instead that an extra one hundred men be added to each infantry battalion, an increase of 4,800 to Corps strength that would give each battalion a strength of 40 officers and 1,066 men. At the same time, Currie argued for the Fifth Canadian Division in England to be dissolved, which was possible because Sam Hughes' malign influence in Ottawa had been weakened since his ouster as Minister of Militia and Defence. Currie succeeded and this provided the necessary infantry for the hundred-man additions, a pool of reinforcements, and well-trained artillery, machine gun, signals, and engineer units. Currie's decisions, based on sound military logic and principle, were the right ones, not least because he sacrificed his own interests for those of his Corps.

Currie's second decision, his insistence that his Corps stay together even through the German offensives that began in March 1918, was similarly based on principle. Occupying positions at Lens and Vimy, the Corps was not directly attacked; however, with the enemy attacking to the north and south, the Canadian position looked more like a salient every day. "And yet the Canadian troops were never in better spirits," wrote Lieutenant Charles Savage after the war. "We were on a front with every inch of which we were thoroughly familiar. The history of Vimy as far as we were concerned was one of success. The position was naturally an exceedingly strong one and that fact also gave us confidence. But what probably really explained our light-heartedness, in a time of somewhat general depression, was the fact that we had not been pounded day after day, week after week, as had the troops that faced the German drives."

At various times, the high command wanted to use the Canadians to plug holes in two different armies and three different corps, or so Currie complained. Although he could not prevent Haig from detaching his divisions for some periods of time, he was able to get them back by mid-April. In essence, Currie was prepared to have his Corps fight as a corps, but not piecemeal. The Canadian division commanders knew each other and their men, they were accustomed to working together because they had trained and fought together from the outset, and their Corps leadership knew how to get the best from them. British divisions,

Trench newspapers provided the soldiers with news. Some regiments printed their own sheets, but the centrally produced *Canadian Daily Record* was the main source for most. DND/LAC

by contrast, floated from corps to corps and ordinarily lacked this familiarity. Currie was a national commander, ultimately responsible to the Canadian government in Ottawa that wanted its men to fight together. He pressed Haig and got his way.

The field marshal was not amused. Currie "lodged a complaint when I ordered the Canadian Divisions to be brought out of the line in order to support the front and take part in the battle elsewhere," Haig fumed in his diary on April 18, adding that General Henry Horne, Currie's army commander, thought the Canadian was "suffering from a swollen head." Haig later added that "I could not help feeling that some people in Canada regard themselves rather as 'allies' than fellow citizens in the Empire." He told the visiting Minister of Militia, Major-General S.C. Mewburn, that "the British Army alone and unaided by Canadian troops, withstood the first terrific blow by 80 German divisions."

Haig was right, but his own less than stellar direction of Britain's Western Front effort had created and dramatically reinforced the nationalist trend in the Canadian Expeditionary Force. General Currie respected Haig, under whom he had served happily through the last 18 months of the war—"one felt that here you were dealing with a thoroughly honest, decent, manly man"—but he had developed the firm conviction that the way the Canadian Corps fought the war was at least as good, if not better, than that practised at Haig's General Headquarters and in the British armies at the front. Certainly he was correct in believing that Canadians fought better when the Corps' divisions were all serving together under Canadian command.

And most Canadian soldiers, whether born in Canada or elsewhere, agreed that their attitude and the way they fought was far better than that of the British. Brooke Claxton, a gunner in the 3rd Brigade and a later Liberal Defence Minister, became a fervent nationalist as a result of his war experience. "We get into a hole," he wrote his father just after the Armistice, "& our feeling is 'come on boys, this ---- thing is in a hole. We've got to get into action as soon as possible so let's get it out and get to bed' & everyone jumps & pulls & heaves and uses his brain." But, he went on, "The Imperial [British soldier] says 'fuck the fucking thing. I'm going to fucking well let it stay in the bloody hole' & it stays."

The Swiss-French artist Théophile Steinlein sketched this kilted and grizzled Canadian soldier in 1918. CWM

Still, the war had to be won, the Canadians were under British command, and the Canadian Corps, rested, fit, and at full strength, trained and readied itself for the next and decisive phase of the struggle.

THREE

BREAKING THE
DROCOURT-QUÉANT LINE

After their great breakthrough at Amiens on August 8, the Canadians began their 40-mile move by bus and train north on August 19, the Second Division being the first to rejoin General Sir Henry Horne's British First Army in the Arras sector. The Third Division followed the next night, and the First and Fourth Divisions a week or more later, arriving on August 25 and 28. Arthur Currie's 100,000-strong Canadian Corps was back near its old lines at Vimy, ready once more to spearhead the First Army's attack.

The sensational success at Amiens, the greatest advance thus far in the war, altered the Allied planning. Now the idea was to maintain the pressure on the enemy with a series of all-out offensives. The French armies attacked between Compiègne and Soissons on August 20. At the same time the British Third Army under General Sir Julian Byng struck toward Bapaume while Rawlinson's Fourth Army, led by the 1st Australian Division, shattered two German divisions on the Somme. Now it was the turn of Horne's First Army and Currie's Canadian Corps to continue the offensive.

Quiet, calm, competent, and close to Haig, Sir Henry Horne had worked frequently and well with Currie and the Canadian Corps. British historian Simon Robbins noted that Horne "clearly admired both the Canadians and their commander," but found the situation somewhat difficult, feeling "hamstrung by the fact that [Currie] was more of an ally than a subordinate." Nonetheless, Horne had no doubts about the Corps' effectiveness. From Vimy onwards, another British historian wrote, "he seems to have acquired the habit of giving all substantial offensive tasks to the Canadian Corps and leaving both planning and execution to that corps' commander and his staff." That Horne did again.

The German positions between Arras and Cambrai in the Scarpe valley's hilly, wooded country consisted of four separate defensive lines, each well designed, fully prepared, and aggressively defended. Immediately in front of the lines occupied by the Second and Third Canadian Divisions was Monchy-le-Preux, a British position lost to the enemy in the offensive of March 1918, and the trenches and strongpoints of the Germans' old front line. Behind these lines was the Fresnes-Rouvray Line, and behind this, blocking the route to Cambrai, the Drocourt-Quéant Line itself. There the Hindenburg Line met the German defences that ran north to Ypres, and the D-Q Line was, in effect, the hinge—a breakthrough there could threaten both defensive zones with being outflanked or rolled up. The Canadian Corps from August 26 to September 2, 1918, had to advance to the D-Q Line and then tackle these well-defended positions that had taken the enemy more than two years to build. The ground had been fought over repeatedly, and the enemy's engineers had made full use of the hills and riverbeds of the Scarpe and Sensée to create what were probably the strongest German defensive positions on the Western Front.

Horne in effect gave Currie command of the entire attack. That made sense because Currie, as Simon Robbins writes, was "the most dynamic and effective of [his] corps commanders," and because the Canadian staff had already begun assessing the German defences in July just before the Corps was diverted south to Amiens. Under the plan as it was finally developed, the British VIII and XXII Corps, the other formations of First Army, were to be used to secure the Canadians' left flank. The main role of Horne's First Army headquarters was to execute a deception plan that used artillery bombardments, dummy installations, and conspicuous infantry-tank training to suggest that the main attack would come north of the Scarpe. In fact, Currie's plan aimed his Corps at the Arras-Cambrai road and, in addition to his two Canadian divisions designated for the initial attack, he had the 51st (Highland) Division under his command.

The Canadians had massive artillery resources at their disposal—14 brigades of field artillery and 9 heavy brigades, much of which was British. Tanks were scarce, however: because of heavy losses and mechanical breakdowns, only 18 were allotted to the two Canadian divisions. Air resources were richer with 13 squadrons including fighters, bombers,

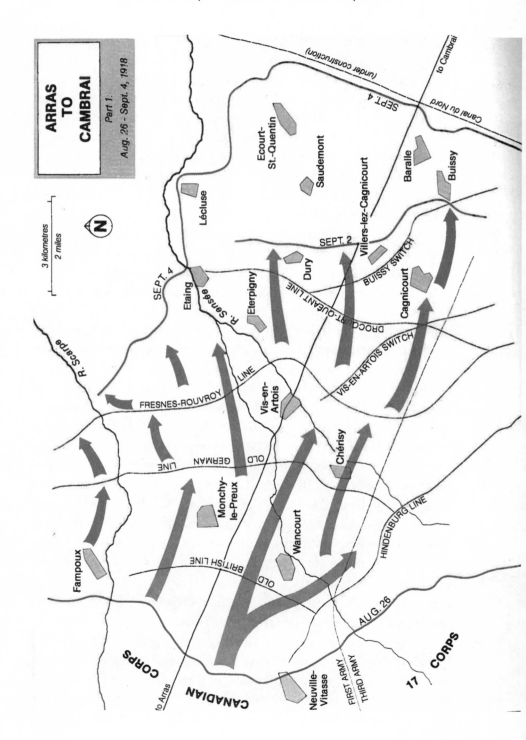

ARRAS TO CAMBRAI

Part 1:
Aug. 26 - Sept. 4, 1918

3 kilometres
2 miles

N

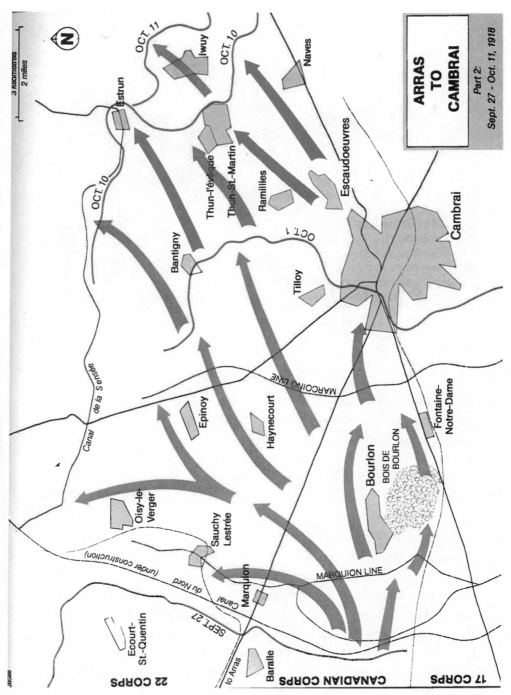

Desmond Morton and J.L. Granatstein, *Marching to Armageddon: Canadians and the Great War 1914–19* (Toronto: Lester & Orpen Dennys, 1989), p. 224–25.

Waiting by the side of the road near Monchy-le-Preux for their orders to advance, soldiers might have sensed that the Germans were faltering. But they knew that there was still hard fighting to come. CWM

and reconnaissance aircraft, and with five squadrons designated to provide close support to the infantry, armour, and cavalry. Zero Hour was 3 a.m. on August 26. That Currie could order a night attack, always one of the most difficult operations in war, was an indication of his complete confidence in his Corps' leaders, staff planners, and men. That attacking at night would hinder the German machine-gunners must also have been a major factor.

The advance depended on the artillery and the few available tanks, but mainly on the infantryman. A few frightened men, advancing under shell fire and bullets, somehow had to worm their way through the enemy's barbed wire to get within bomb-throwing range of a machine gun. If they were lucky or very skillful, they could eliminate it and move forward a few more yards to the next emplacement. But it was a risky business of kill or be killed; too often it was kill *and* be killed.

A young lieutenant in the 1st Canadian Mounted Rifles, Ivan Maharg fought in his first battle that day. It was, he wrote home, not a case of into the line to hold the trench, but rather, over the top after only one hour in the front line & rush in the dark & on into daylight right through until noon. In this time we found that we had reached our final objective & had pushed forward five miles. Gee, but it was sure some initiation for me, but the hardest part of it all was that first single hour of waiting until our barage [*sic*] opened up at 3 a.m. and we jumped off. . . . As well as our artillery barrage our Divisional Machine Gun battalion put up their barrage too.

The Germans had been expecting an attack by the Canadians—"the best British troops," the enemy called them—but the deception plan and the start time in the middle of the night caught them by surprise. By 6 a.m., Major-General H.E. Burstall's Second Division had taken Chapel Hill, and the Third Division under Major-General L.J. Lipsett had Orange Hill and Monchy-le-Preux by 7:40. The fighting had been bloody. The 116th Battalion in the Third Division took its first objective and then lost it three times before finally reaching its goal. The unit lost its acting commanding officer and some 300 officers and men in two days of action.

One young officer in the 20th Battalion in the Second Division, Lieutenant R.C. Germain, wrote home from hospital of the fighting. "We were held up by machine gun fire from a ridge in front. We had got into the Boche transport lines. What do you think they did?" he asked. "They tied their horses, placed machine guns under the horses' bellies and fired point blank into us." Germain said he lost half his company, but the survivors "rushed them and they had the nerve to throw up their hands and cry, 'Kamerad.' All the 'Kamerad' they got was a foot of cold steel thro them from my remaining men while I blew their brains out with my revolver without any hesitation." He added for his mother's sake, "You may think this rather rough but if you had seen my boys go down you would have done the same."

The fighting to get through the German positions in front of the D-Q Line itself was fierce. Supported by their artillery, German counterattacks later in the day were beaten back, though they forestalled any additional advance, and by nightfall the Canadians held a thousand-yard line about three miles ahead of their jumping-off position. The cost had been high in killed and wounded.

The Royal Air Force had played its part. Gavin Baird, a bomber pilot, recollected his role in attacking enemy positions at Monchy-le-Preux:

> We were cooperating with the infantry in obliterating several very strong machine gun nests. The artillery had been hammering at them, but every time the infantry went to advance they were met with a stubborn resistance. Our entire squadron bombed one very little town on [the Arras-Cambrai] road one night and most of the machines made three trips, so you can imagine what was left of that town in the morning. We heard later that the infantry walked through and any German that was left alive was so dazed that he could hardly give a coherent statement.

This infantry-air cooperation would have been almost inconceivable a year earlier, but by the battles of August 1918 it was almost routine.

Lieutenant Maharg's diary account captured the essence of the Third Division's attack. "Advance to Monchy. McDonaugh and Riault killed. Zero hour goes at 3 a.m. Dandy barage [sic] opens on time & away they

Strafing aircraft took a heavy toll on troops in the field. Enemy machine-gunners, ordinarily the most determined German soldiers, were a particular target, as they were here east of Arras in September 1918. DND/LAC

go." Maharg's A Company of the 1st Canadian Mounted Rifles "moves out at zero + 75 minutes. Moved my platoon forward in Artillery formation under heavy machine gun fire from Mount Pleasant on our left flank. Reached our final objective by 8 a.m. after going about 4 miles. B, C, & D Coys all disorganized. . . . B,C & D on through Monchy but had to fall back. 9th Bgde too late to leap frog & Hun has chance to regain himself." For the next two days, Maharg's 1st CMR was largely at rest or in support, but he had survived his first battle when many of his colleagues had not. As he noted, all the officers in one of his battalion's four companies had been killed or wounded.

When he wrote home on August 30, Maharg seemed both more matter-of-fact and cheerful:

> The Hun seemed to be depending upon the large number of his machine guns rather than his artillery to hold us back. About 1/3 of the distance to our objective we came under heavy machine gun fire just crossing a high ridge known as "Orange hill." The "Imperials" on our left (across the Scarpe river) were much slower in there [sic] advance than ourselves & the hun was firing from a wood across the river right into our left flank. We at once sized up the situation & hurried forward & down into the valley.

There were casualties, but by this point the enemy "seemed absolutely up in the air & was evacuating & leaving everything behind in his endeavour to escape. . . . The opposition seemed so slight that the company instead of stopping pushed on past the town & into the open." At that point resistance stiffened, the Canadians fell back, and, Maharg noted, his unit had about a hundred casualties, including seven officers killed and four wounded.

Bertie Cox, the gunner from Winnipeg, wrote home on August 29 to report that he had just returned from a souvenir hunt in the newly liberated German dugouts. "It's great sport. . . . There's all kinds of stuff, but of course the Infantry grab the best of it and they are always there ahead of us," he said. He had gone into one dugout "about 50 ft. deep, fitted up as a forward dressing station. Bundles of bandages and dope to put in wounds etc. etc. All kinds of medical apparatus." Rob Shortreed, a gunner from Edmonton, wrote two weeks after Cox that he was living in a German dugout with "two or three entrances each with about forty steps leading down and then runs about 100 feet or more underground with little chambers off at the sides. It is all six feet clear and solid chalk walls so you can imagine the labour to build."

Another soldier, Charles Savage, spoke similarly about the enemy's dugouts:

> The German dugouts that we occupied were exceedingly well made and most comfortable. It was our first experience of the safety and luxury of such shelters and we appreciated them to the utmost. We also wondered why we had never had any of our own. Some dugouts that had been used by the Germans as Divisional or Corps Headquarters were elaborate suites of

The Germans constructed their dugouts and gun positions of concrete, intending them to be "permanent." It took fierce fighting to dislodge them from this emplacement at Monchy-le-Preux. CWM

In what was likely a posed shot, this Canadian cyclist is calling on German defenders to surrender and emerge from their dugout located east of Arras. A dead soldier lies nearby. DND/LAC

rooms with wooden floors and with ceilings and walls carefully papered or painted. There were bedrooms, dining rooms, living rooms, offices, kitchens, pantries, etc; in fact they were regular underground houses. Some of them even had electric lights and bathrooms. Of course, such palatial lodgings were for the Staff; but our accommodations, though not so luxurious, were equally safe, and we certainly had no complaints to make about them.

Neither Shortreed nor Cox said, but might have done (as Savage did), that the enemy dugouts were always deeper, stronger, and better fitted out than British and Canadian ones. The Germans, generally on the defensive, built their strongpoints for keeps; the Allies, ordinarily attacking, somehow believed that if their positions were more comfortable and durable, the troops would lose their offensive élan.

The next two days of fighting in front of the D-Q Line were less successful than the first. Heavy rain grounded the Royal Air Force and made the terrain slippery, and the advances were small, each gain paid for in lives as the troops ran into uncut wire, heavy artillery, machine-gun fire, and stubborn defenders. Casualties over the three days of operations totalled 5,801, and some battalions were almost wiped out. The 22nd, the sole French-Canadian unit in the Corps, lost all its officers—including the later Governor-General Major Georges Vanier who, while acting as commanding officer, was hit in the stomach and then, while being attended to by a stretcher bearer, was wounded once more. His right leg had to be amputated. General Currie later called the Corps' advance to the D-Q Line "the hardest battle in its history." The losses were grievous, but the gains had been impressive: a five-mile advance over difficult country that had been stoutly defended. The Canadians had taken 3,300 prisoners and much equipment, but the Second and Third Divisions were tired, worn-out, and in need of rest and reinforcements. Currie had to pull them out of the line and put the First and Fourth Canadian Divisions and the British 4th Division into action for the next operation.

The Canadian Corps' mission now was to crack the Drocourt-Quéant Line itself. The enemy's defences here consisted of a front line and a support line, both with many concrete bunkers and machine-gun posts. The front system, located on the forward slope, gave good fields of fire; the support trenches were sited on reverse slopes for maximum protection. The Buissy Switch, connecting the D-Q Line to the Hindenburg Line, had been built to similar standards, and it ran along the forward slope of Mont Dury, itself a position bristling with machine-gun nests and with German artillery sited behind the hill.

General Currie decided to go "all out." He scheduled the attack for September 2, and his plan was to hit at the Arras-Marquion road and then swing both north and south, rolling up the enemy defences. The British Third Army would attack on the right, tying down German reserves; the left flank rested on marshland and the support of First Army. The attack by three divisions—the British 4th with one of the smaller British brigades up, the Fourth and First Canadian each with two of the stronger Canadian brigades up—had massive artillery support, 20 brigades of field artillery and 11 of the heavies. The heavy guns were to

Getting through the German defences was always costly. The enemy's all-but-impregnable bunkers were well-constructed—steel and concrete—and the interlocked fields of fire tested the attackers' determination. This machine-gun bunker on the Drocourt-Quéant Line was but one example. DND/LAC

isolate the battlefield and do counter-battery work; the field guns' task was to lay down a rolling barrage moving forward a hundred yards every three minutes until it reached the forward edge of the D-Q Line, at which point it would slow. After two-and-a-half hours, the barrage was to stop moving—but continue firing—for 30 minutes so the attackers could consolidate their gains to fend off the anticipated German counterattacks. There were also two companies of Mark V tanks and lavish air support that faced off against the enemy air force and, as it turned out, suffered heavy losses—36 aircraft shot down against one German casualty. German aircraft also strafed Canadian troops during the day.

The Canadian Corps' attack jumped off at 5 a.m. on a front of 7,000 yards. The troops ran into the seven German divisions facing them and the British Third Army to their south. Some of the opposition crumpled quickly under the weight of the artillery attack—ten thousand tons fired between August 27 and September 2—and the quick movement of the infantry and tanks. But at Mont Dury, the Germans resisted fiercely, inflicting heavy casualties on the Fourth Division. On the First Division front, the Buissy Switch was the objective, and the attack was led by the 10th Battalion.

A long diary account by Captain Jack Andrews, a Winnipeg lawyer before the war who had been promoted from the ranks in 1916, conveyed the utter confusion, total chaos, and raw courage of the 10th Battalion's action on September 2:

> We moved off at 2:15AM on Sept 2 to an assembly position on a hill. I had "C" Co. who were in reserve to the Battalion. We got placed in a deep dugout where we stayed until 5 AM (Zero Hour). There was a heavy [German] bombardment prior to the attack but we lost no men as all were under cover. We had no idea of the country and were following tapes that had been laid down. At 5 AM the attack on Buissy Switch started. We followed battalion headquarters as reserve. As it moved so we moved. At one point a shell fell at my feet but it was a dud. Finally the attack stopped and we dug in under a bank just outside Vis-en-Artois. Gradually my company was used up as reinforcements to the other companies who had suffered pretty badly. Finally Carey O[fficer]. C[ommanding]. of "B" Co. was wounded in the stomach and I was sent up to take over his company. The O.C. called me in and said we would attack Buissy Switch just west of Vis-en-Artois at 6:30 and an artillery barrage (very small) would precede the attack. It was 4 PM when I was ordered up. I found two platoons with Capt. Graham. . . . I explained the attack and went to "A" Co Lt. McEacheran in command but couldn't find him but explained to his 2nd in command and we agreed that he with 6 platoons and 2 of mine who were under his command would attack the switch while I with 2 platoons would cover the open [flank] to the 3rd Brigade who were in front of Hendecourt. I had previously arranged that if I didn't get back by 6:20 that Graham was to take command. They had told me of a machine gun half right and I left instructions to get a gun from the 1st Batt. who were in reserve to us to cover our advance.

When I got back, I found Graham had forgotten the gun, so I ran back to get one and by the time I got back the troops had started. I ran after them but a barrage was laid down, and my men ran for the trench. I shouted to them but only about 15 came. . . . We spread out and connected with the 3rd Brigade. While there . . . a row started in the switch and I said to the 3rd Brigade officer, that is our boys taking the switch. He laughed and said that it couldn't be done. After things quieted down I returned to Batt. Hqrs with my 15 men and put them in a dugout and reported to headquarters. On the way I met McEacheran with a number of prisoners. He said he had taken the switch. . . . I asked about my company and he said he knew nothing about them. We both saw Col. MacDonald. McEacheran told his story and then the O.C. asked about "B" Co. I couldn't report for anything except 15 men. The O.C. ordered me to bed and told Capt. Costello to take over my company. I was in disgrace . . . I couldn't sleep and went to Major Ferguson. He refused to see me, said I was a disgrace and had been relieved.

Nothing in this account suggested a smoothly operating crack unit with well-trained officers and men. Nor did anything seem to have gone right for Andrews personally who was likely treated unjustly, but the important point was that the 10th Battalion had reached its objective and taken the Buissy Switch.

Fighting continued through dusk on September 2 and into the 3rd. Captain Andrews, apparently forgiven his sins of the 2nd, was ordered to take command of B Company again

and move off at noon to conform with an attack of the 4th Division on our left. No written orders [.] I was sent to support "A" Co. I went up and went to "A" Co. to report our orders. We moved off and at a point about 1 mile N.W. of Buissy "A" Co. turned half left. I ran up to McEacheran and told him he should go straight on. He didn't agree so I went straight ahead, in front of my Co. We crossed the railway track and just as we got in sight of the canal or rather a small stream running at right angles to the Canal-du-Nord the Germans opened with 4.1 and machine gun. We dropped and I got into a shell hole and got out my glasses. In front was the canal or stream and there wasn't another piece of shelter on its bank. As I looked the bridge was blown up by the Germans. I then passed along word to retire and line the railway bank. The men got back in ones and twos. . . . I remained out in front to observe till I was sent for by Major Ferguson. When I got back I found the 1st Battalion lining the railway, so I pulled out my company and found a dugout just in support of "A" Co. It turned out [McEacheran] was right after all and I had been in the 1st Battalion area. I never thought we would get out alive when they caught us on the forward slope of the hill above the canal. McEacheran was wounded and my batman [the officer's soldier-servant] killed by the barrage.

Andrews concluded his epic of the confusion, casualties, and chaos that had characterized the assault of September 3: "At night we were relieved by the 7th and marched back to Villers Cognicourt. We were lost part of the time. It was new ground but we finally arrived. One of the officers had to go back and find his platoon."

Canadians developed counter-battery operations to a high art. This German gun, destroyed east of Buissy in September, was one of many to fall victim to the Canadian gunners. DND/LAC

And yet, despite all the muddle, it was a substantial victory. The Canadians took some 6,000 prisoners and killed or wounded thousands more. There was also much courage on display. One young officer remembered his commanding officer, Lieutenant-Colonel Cy Peck of the 16th Battalion, "walking in the open, under fire, his kilt riddled and spare holster shot through, with his hands on his breeches, calmly reorganizing his men and driving them forward." Peck, elected a Union Government Member of Parliament for Skeena, B.C., in December 1917, won the Victoria Cross for his actions that day. A big fat man with a walrus mustache, he was almost certainly the first sitting M.P. to do so, and among the very few men anywhere to hold the Victoria Cross and the Distinguished Service Order and bar. Other soldiers in the 14th Battalion recalled leaving a just-captured village only to confront a horse-drawn enemy artillery battery galloping into view. Fire from their Lewis guns brought the battery to a halt—and to surrender.

The two Canadian divisions in the attack had lost 297 officers and 5,325 other ranks, most of the dead and wounded as always coming from the less than 25,000 infantry in the 24 battalions. In truth, the ten battalions that had spearheaded the attack were almost annihilated. Such losses of experienced and well-trained soldiers could not be sustained for long, and the morale of the Canadians, though buoyed by their victories, was fragile. Earl Bolton, a private from Ingersoll, Ontario, wrote his sister on September 22 "just a few lines to let you know I am still alive. Things are pretty lively here with us. We are sure giving Fritz all he wants now. I have been in one scrap and just out on rest getting ready for another. . . . my friend was killed in the last push which makes it pretty lonesome for me. . . . You never know what minute you are a dead man here. Shells burst around you that would blowup a building the size of a house." Bolton was wounded ten days later and died on October 9.

Clarence Gass, a lieutenant in the 85th Battalion in the Fourth Division, was both more cheerful and more successful in surviving the war. He wrote his wife on September 9 about the D-Q Line battles, calling them "the hardest scrap I've ever been through. I was very fortunate as I came out without a scratch. The battalion had the honour of taking one of the hardest parts of the line and the boys sure did the job well." He added that his men "got all kinds of souvenirs but the only thing I brought back was a very fine automatic revolver. I had the satisfaction of 'getting' two of the blonde brutes. At least I am sure of two and I think I got several more." Gass noted that he had been given his old platoon once more but "there are only a few left that were with me in the old days."

Captain Fred Banting, later the co-discoverer of insulin, was the medical officer of the 44th Battalion in the Fourth Canadian Division. On September 2, he wrote in his diary that he had set up his Regimental Aid Post in a "Hun Dressing Station" near Dury "using their dressings and Red Cross Flag. . . . The wounded poured in and I kept eighteen bearers and twenty to thirty Huns carrying [wounded] out. A couple of nice Heinies worked around all day." Glad to be alive, prisoners very often helped their captors, and assisting a medical officer with the wounded—usually including German wounded—accorded with even the most punctilious soldier's ideas of how war should be fought. Always there were more than enough casualties to require everyone to help.

Still, the rewards of the Canadian attack on the D-Q Line genuinely seemed to be worth the dreadful cost. By midday on September 2 the

A famous photograph shows captured Germans carrying Canadian wounded to the rear while a huge tank belches fumes. CWM

German high command had already decided to retire eastward to take up positions behind the Sensée River and the Canal du Nord. German armies to the north and south were also ordered to retire to better defence lines, the enemy thus giving up all the territory gained in the offensives of March and April. Battered as they were, the German armies still could surprise. Their withdrawal on the Canadian front to positions behind the Canal du Nord, the line that Captain Chambers' company of the 10th Battalion had bumped into, was brilliantly handled. When the Corps' troops advanced on September 3, some moving forward behind creeping barrages, they discovered only empty dugouts. The Canadian victory on the D-Q Line was a real one, but the enemy remained far from beaten.

"Tough battles cost lives," British historian Christopher Pugsley observed, "and Currie was both mindful of the cost and prepared to fight his divisions to win—in 1918 there was no other easy way." Currie truly grieved at the losses, but he was buoyant when he offered special praise to his First Division, calling its actions on September 2 in assaulting and taking the Fresnes-Rouvray and Drocourt-Quéant Lines "one of the finest performances in all the war." He wrote on September 3 in his diary that "it is a question whether our victory of yesterday or of August 8th is the greatest, but I am inclined to think yesterday's was." Few would disagree, wrote the official historian of the Canadian Expeditionary Force. "The Corps' success in destroying the hinge of the German defence system had not only made it possible for the Third Army to advance; the repercussions were to be felt along the whole front."

Those in command of the Allied armies recognized the significance of these events. Field Marshal Haig and Marshal Foch met on October 6. Foch held up the Paris newspapers with headlines shouting that the enemy were looking for an armistice. "Here," Foch said, "there is the immediate result of the British piercing of the Hindenburg Line." The British and Canadian soldiers, smashing through the toughest German defences, had forced the enemy to seek terms.

The Canadian Corps' victories had much to do with its logistics. Without the capacity to supply and sustain the infantry, engineers, signallers, and artillery at the front, the Corps could neither advance nor retreat. General

Currie, the organizer of victory, had learned from his experiences from April 1915 onwards, and he worked hard to create an effective and efficient behind-the-lines operation.

Some months prior to the victory at Amiens in August 1918, the Corps' Supply Column and the Canadian Corps Ammunition Park were amalgamated to form the Headquarters Canadian Corps Mechanical Transport [MT] Column. Under this headquarters from April onwards were the Corps Troops MT Company, a Divisional MT Company for each of the four divisions, a Motor Machine Gun MT Company, and an Engineer MT Company. The divisional companies drew the supplies and ammunition their divisions required, and in July 1918, just before the Hundred Days, the Canadian Corps added a Motor Machine Gun MT Company and a Canadian Engineer MT Company, the latter the largest column in the Corps responsible for transporting stores required by the Corps' large complement of engineers. In all, this gave Currie's Corps one hundred more trucks than its British counterparts, a big advantage.

The number of engineers in the Corps also had been increased substantially to more than 3,000 in each of the four divisions, and the Canadian Engineers could now provide most of the labour needed to

Rapidly moving troops and supplies, especially artillery shells, was a major task for the BEF, and the Canadians proved to be expert in constructing light rail lines. This effort was underway near Vimy in 1917. DND/LAC

perform assigned tasks, rather than begging for labour from infantry units. There was also a Bridging Transport Unit, designed to be able to put down a pontoon bridge of up to 225 feet: this was very necessary in France, cut as it was by many rivers. And there were two Tramway Companies, building, maintaining, and operating narrow-gauge rail lines that the Corps had pioneered and raised to a high art. During the Hundred Days, as at Vimy, these lines proved extraordinarily useful in bringing supplies forward.

Currie understood the necessity of having labour battalions for various tasks. The infantrymen needed rest when out of the line, not to be put to work on construction of roads or digging trenches. After April 1918, a Canadian Works Group Headquarters commanded four infantry works companies used to dig trenches, construct rail lines, build roads, handle ammunition, and other essential tasks. Each division also had an employment company to provide extra labour, and five Canadian Area Employment Companies provided labour for rear-area tasks. There were also pioneer battalions, including one, the 107th, largely manned by First Nations soldiers who could undertake specialized construction tasks and double as infantry. In effect, the Corps had the mechanical transport and labour pools it needed to handle the needs of an elite fighting force. More was better, and the Canadian Corps had more of everything.

The effectiveness of this new organization was demonstrated in the clandestine move of the Canadian Corps from the area of Arras to Amiens at the end of July and early August 1918. To transfer a hundred thousand men, thousands of vehicles, horses, guns, ammunition, and supplies was an incredible task, made more so by the short notice the logistics staff received. The Corps' Senior MT Officer received his warning order only the day before the move was to begin, his first task being to load ammunition on every empty truck moving south so that an ammunition dumping program could begin immediately after arrival at Amiens. Meanwhile, the Corps headquarters was shifted 80 miles in one day by the Engineers MT Company. The Second Division, to give only one example, beginning on July 29 moved by a combination of rail, buses, and on foot, and completed the transfer on the 31st. Much of the movement was accomplished at night to maintain secrecy, an extra complication.

Shells were heavy and fired in huge quantities. Getting them to the guns required much logistical planning, trains, trucks, and strong men. CWM

Inevitably, there were problems. Lieutenant-Colonel W.B. Anderson, the assistant quartermaster general of the Corps, complained of the short notice his organization had received. He noted that the Third Division almost failed to receive its trench munitions and had none until the night of August 7, only a few hours before the Amiens attack began. If his staff had known of the operation earlier, he argued, arrangements for the full range of logistical details necessary for a major attack could have been perfected. And Anderson pointed out that staff officers were far less likely to breach secrecy than were the thousands of horses being led to watering points three times a day prior to the battle.

Once the attack began, priority had to be given to get "communications across No Man's Land at the earliest possible moment to enable the Field Artillery to get forward." Divisional transport was restricted to roads and tracks in its own areas only, and the Fourth Division (in reserve) alone was permitted to make use of any convenient roads when it needed to get forward. But there were problems with the control of the divisional transport companies and with the delivery of ammunition, in substantial part because the British Expeditionary Force controlled the railway trains that brought artillery shells forward to the Corps' railheads. The cause, the senior MT officer said, "was not the lack of transport or the service that was rendered by the lorries, but the supply." As it was, the Corps' MT had to bring 2,000 tons of ammunition to forward battle positions each night in a gruelling journey. General Currie had insisted that his MT drivers were physically fit; this was clearly necessary as only such men could have done the job. Complicating matters further was a petrol shortage in the British Fourth Army area that immobilized many trucks. The last deliveries of shells were made just before Zero Hour on August 8.

On the Third Division front, the attacking infantry had to cross the River Luce, using bridges built by the engineers. Will Bird, an infantryman and later a well-known writer, wrote that on August 8 "there was a thick mist . . . but someone had foreseen such a difficulty and there was a strand of wire strung . . . from the trenches to the bridges. We could not hurry in the least, as the pontoon bridge was swaying under the tread of those crossing. Some shells landed with great splashes in the river [but] . . . Our platoon made it without a hitch." Heavier bridges were built for MT vehicles and tanks, including the supply tanks that carried ammunition and supplies forward (though only at one mile per hour).

The very success of the Amiens assault tested the logistical system to the greatest extent. To keep the advance going required ammunition and vast quantities of supplies of all kinds, a feat complicated by the additional distance the goods had to be transported. That the feat was accomplished as well as it was confirmed that the elite Canadian Corps' supply and transport organization was up to the challenge, as efficient in its own sphere as the fighting arms.

Food was a key element of the soldiers' lives, as essential as ammunition. Canadians were not gourmets before the Great War, and soldiers, like civilians, had a diet that was heavy on meat, potatoes, bread, and tea or water. Lieutenant Ivan Maharg of the 1st Canadian Mounted Rifles wrote in August 1918 that he was his regiment's officers' mess president. He himself had just had "a good lunch of Pork & Beans, Tomatoes & potatoes, also sago pudding bread & tea. Even with that," he said, "the

Gunners from the 1st Canadian Siege Battery, wearing forage caps as an indication they were not expecting immediate action, lunch under their camouflage netting. CWM

officers are kicking at me for not feeding them fresh meat. . . . I have just given our 'caterer' [presumably the sergeant who looked after the officers' messing] 20 francs to see if he can't find us some eats in this village. I doubt if he can, there's not much here." Officers ordinarily contributed a portion of their pay for "extra messing," but even without meat, Maharg and his messmates received sufficient calories to keep them going.

The Corps' soldiers, of course, did not pay for their food. Bert Lovell of the 8th Canadian Field Ambulance recalled what happened when his unit was on the march:

Our cooks have the Mulligan Batteries [i.e., the cookstoves] going as we march northward. The bread comes in jute sacks and the cooks save the broken pieces. . . . Bright idea of the cooks, give the boys "Bread Pudding" so into the kettle goes the broken bread that has been bumping against the wagon all day, some raisins, sugar, and "voila" bread pudding with tea, cheese and jam. Ah, what a feast. The jute fibres cling to the bread so that the bread pudding would have made good plaster. . . . Sgt. Davis, head cook, waves our complaints away with his usual "If you don't like it, see 'King George.'"

Infantry units in the front line had their rations brought forward from the supply dump and distributed throughout the battalion by companies and platoons. Early in the war, small groups of men ordinarily cooked their food over a "tommy cooker," a small camp stove fuelled by solidified alcohol, and shared it out. Later, company cooks cooked the rations centrally, delivering hot meals to the trenches in insulated containers. There was often tinned jam of an indefinable kind, bread, some stew, or bacon. The history of the 116th Battalion noted that just before the attack toward Cambrai on September 27, 1918, the unit had bivouacked in shell holes "with no covering except waterproof sheets and no hot dinner. About 3 a.m. the next morning the kitchens arrived, and the men gathered round them in small groups to try and get warm. It is surprising how good a thick bacon sandwich is with a ration of rum at 5 o'clock in the morning." Canned beef, another staple, was frequently gristle and fat, whether from Argentina, the United States, or Harris Abattoir, a Toronto meat-packing house. Water came forward in gasoline cans and was frequently in short supply, especially in hot weather. Drinking water from local sources, frequently contaminated, was discouraged. Better to have the men drink boiled tea—nothing harmful could survive in that.

Daily rations were supplemented by parcels from home that contained luxuries such as cake, candies, canned salmon, or tinned fruit. Roy Macfie in the 1st Battalion wrote home that he had just eaten "a lot of candies and a big piece of dandy fruit cake all the way from Canada." That parcel might have been his, but it was as likely as not that it was from one of his platoon mates who shared it around. That was the proper thing to do. A soldier who kept the goodies to himself would be scorned.

An officer's food, cooked by a batman, or personal servant, when in the trenches usually was individually prepared. Maharg's account catches the flavour of the experience:

I wish you could have seen my poor servant trying to get me a meal under fire. For a day & a half it was easy as we were down a dry dug-out & he could cook with ease. At other times he'd try to get me a pot of tea where he happened to pause in some trench or shell hole. Once he had a pretty fair looking meal ready to give me when a big shell burst so close that he kicked over the tea & spilt some bacon he was trying to fry. On another occasion, he was all ready when the order suddenly came in to move forward. . . . no meal was had that time either.

The other ranks, no one to cook their meals, had to wait for the cooks to send the food forward.

Almost all this food had to be shipped from Britain and brought up the British Expeditionary Force's supply chain from Boulogne and four other ports to front-line units. This amounted monthly, in the case of Boulogne alone, to more than 21 million pounds of meat and almost 16 million pounds of bread. Each division—and the BEF had 64 in the field by the autumn of 1918—required an entire train load of supplies (including ammunition and other necessities) each day. Trucks from the division's Canadian Army Service Corps supply column met the train at the railhead and delivered bulk supplies to each brigade. There it was divided into unit allotments, and battalion quartermasters sent their wagons to pick up the rations which were then divided into platoon portions. Each evening at dusk, the company quartermaster sergeant took the wagon forward and ration parties picked up their food, never forgetting the rum jar. The food came in jute bags—tea, sugar, meat, vegetables, and a three-pound loaf of bread for each three men. If the unit was in hard fighting with high casualties, the survivors might eat heartily. But if the enemy were attacking, they might go hungry, forced to eat their iron rations of hardtack and tinned beef. The aim was to provide each soldier with 4,300 calories a day, a recognition that fighting a war was hard labour. It must have worked: the average soldier gained six pounds during his military service.

Supplying the front with food was a massive task that strained the logistical system. The Canadian Corps, like some others, operated farms of its own to produce rations, mainly vegetables, nearer the front.

On the home front, Canadians were exhorted to not waste food that could feed troops overseas. Canada was a huge wartime exporter of grains and meat. DND/LAC

Purchasing officers bought what they could in France as well, and whenever they had the chance, most often when they were out of the line, soldiers scrounged—stole—what they could from farmers' barns or fields, got a free bowl of soup or stew from the "Sally Ann" (the Salvation Army's canteens, located as far forward as possible), or purchased meals in *estaminets,* or local cafés, where they might be able to get "vin blanc" or "eggs and chips" for the nominal sum of two francs.

No one ate well in the trenches, but the soldiers received the calories they needed. Few ate very well out of the trenches either, but again there was usually enough. And when units did not get their full rations or received them late, the complaints were fierce. The supply lines usually went unnoticed, and they are often beneath the notice of historians, but without their efficient functioning the entire operation would have ground to a halt. The Canadian Corps, like every other army, marched on its stomach.

Once, after Amiens, the Canadian Corps again moved north to Arras (another logistical feat); once it broke through the Drocourt-Quéant Line and crossed the Canal du Nord; once its advance speeded up through October and into November 1918; and once the Canadians moved into Germany on occupation duties, the logistical demands on the Corps' supply and transport system would become even greater.

FOUR

CROSSING THE CANAL DU NORD AND TAKING CAMBRAI

After breaking the Drocourt-Quéant Line, the men of Sir Arthur Currie's Canadian Corps enjoyed a well-earned rest. There was time to bring up reinforcements—after a major battle like Amiens or the D-Q Line, the new men always made up a quarter to a half of infantry battalion strength, and they needed to be integrated into their platoons and regiments. Some officers went on leave, going to Paris or London or to a Corps Officers Rest Hostel near Boulogne. Fewer other ranks were given leave, but some did get to England. Many units mounted concerts, featuring female impersonators, ribald songs, and skits that poked fun— sometimes bitter fun—at their officers.

Most men close behind the front simply lay about, lingered over their daily tot of rum, and hoped to avoid the German artillery shells that regularly came over the lines (and caused about a hundred casualties a day), or watching the dogfights in the sky. "Yesterday was a clear day," one gunner wrote on September 16, "and I have never before seen so much aerial activity. Could easily see forty of our planes at one time and they were lively. Saw several fights and some of the enemy machines forced to the ground and also several balloons going up in flames."

As they relaxed, soldiers read and reread the letters from their families and sweethearts in Canada. Mail from home was vitally important, and it could be and usually was delivered quickly. Few soldiers could write more often than once a week—some were illiterate and needed a friend to write letters for them—and most correspondence was banal in the extreme, hiding the details of combat to talk of the friends they had made in France or England or the sights they had seen. Many numbered their own letters so family could keep track, and all loved receiving mail, reading about the details of who was getting married or had a baby. Some

Regimental or division concert parties formed in many parts of the Canadian Corps. Some were mainly satirical, poking at the officers and NCOs. Others aimed for nostalgia. Almost all featured female impersonators, evoking the companionship soldiers missed most. CWM

heard of the deaths of grandparents and parents and other tragedies, and many soldiers received a "Dear John" from a faithless girlfriend or sometimes a wayward spouse. Mail connected soldiers to home, usually bolstered morale, and it gave the news, good and bad.

Sometimes, it was news of the politics on the home front, and the soldiers talked about it all. "No debating society ever had more earnest speakers than I have heard," wrote Sergeant T.C. Lapp. The men, he went on, had read the stories of food shortages in Canada, but this received little sympathy: "Let 'em try European rations for a year." As for the labour situation in Canada,

> The numerous strikes and threatening strikes cause great irritation. It is incomprehensible to us that a man earning $7.50 a day, with all the comforts of home and family, should choose a time of crisis to ask for a 100 percent increase, such as some C.P.R. men have recently done. Compared to $1.10 a day in a hole in the ground under constant shell fire, the majority of working men at home are enjoying the extreme of luxury.

The gap between the soldiers and the Canadian public, the gap that would lead to most returned men opposing the Winnipeg General Strike and other labour unrest in 1919, was becoming very clear.

For one thing, soldiers in the trenches and out swore continuously. They used military lingo, all but incomprehensible to civilians. They looked for "cushy" jobs where they would not be required to show a "chit" to their sergeant and where they wouldn't get "cooties" or worry about "whiz-bangs" and "potato mashers." Maybe they could even escape the "M&V," the tinned slop of meat and vegetables they were fed so often.

They naturally talked often about women, their language frequently crude and foul. Thomas Dinesen, a Dane serving in the 42nd Battalion and a Victoria Cross winner, wrote after the war that he had been appalled by his comrades who were willing to "use any trick . . . to get what they want" from a woman they wanted to bed, "and then beat it." They would not give their name or regimental number, hiding them "from her when leaving so that they themselves are quite on the safe side should some consequence or other ensue from their actions." In France, licensed brothels serviced the troops—"blue lamps" for officers, "red lamps" for other ranks—at a cost of some 10 francs. (There was a story that a brothel in Le Havre employed one lady who wore a British officer's uniform and was much in demand as a result among disrespectful soldiers.) The Canadians always seemed to manage to contract the highest rates of venereal disease in the British Expeditionary Force—209.4 cases per thousand in Britain in 1916, approximately 150 cases per thousand in France, and 66,000 cases during the entire war. Perhaps this was because the Canadians were simple lads, unversed in the wiles of European women. One soldier, Percy McClare, wrote home that he was shocked by the ladies of London who "will come up to you . . . and they will take you by the arm and want you to go home with [them] and stay all night with them." McClare's morality notwithstanding, the Canadians' high VD rate was not a sign of a well-disciplined force, and some diseased prostitutes in England were said to be paid to infect soldiers, thus keeping them out of the trenches.

On the other hand, many soldiers (including General Currie) brought their wives and children to England, some 30,000 by early 1917. Others fell in love and married women they met in Britain, France, or Belgium. For example, Major Maurice Pope, a staff officer who rose very high in the army before and during the Second World War, married a Belgian countess he met after the Armistice. Others wed women of all classes, from army nurses they met in convalescent hospitals to scullery maids. Many served long enough overseas to begin families, and more than 37,000 wives and children came to Canada from Britain alone after the war.

When they were out of the line, soldiers might get the chance to wash if they were billeted on a farm or in a house with running water, which was then much rarer in France or Belgium than it is today. In the trenches, where water was rationed and intended for drinking, soldiers had little chance to clean up or shave. But out of the line, units could be paraded to a baths unit for a shower and a change of clothing, the glorious chance to wash away the filth and lice accumulated by days or weeks of living in holes in the ground. There were rats in all the trenches, feeding on food or, more terribly, corpses. They also carried fleas, as did the many dogs that wandered into rear areas or the trench lines and became pets for soldiers craving affection. The fleas soon lived on the soldiers, as did the lice that thrived in the seams of uniform clothing or body hair. The men fought against these itchy, blood-sucking "cooties," but they usually lost these battles until they received their infrequent showers and fresh clothing.

Bert Lovell who served with the 8th Canadian Field Ambulance amusingly recalled a "bath parade":

Soldiers loved pets, often strays they found wandering in the ruins of villages. This dog and some displaced civilian's pet monkey became the regimental mascot of the 8th Battalion, CEF. DND/LAC

At home bath night is usually Saturday night, over there it was any old time, and not too often. The bath houses were rigged up by the [Canadian Engineers] usually in an old factory where there was water. The equipment was a boiler and a room with a wooden floor, with several faucets in the ceiling. Adjacent to this was the room where one left his dirty clothing and filed into the bathroom where several bars of English soap were on the floor. When as many men as could be crowded in (something like the Black Hole of Calcutta) the engineer would cry in a loud voice "water on" and streams of water would cascade from above. This would shut off. Then the voice would cry "soap on" [and] at once each man would grab a bar of soap and vigorously soap his body and do the back of his neighbour. Then the voice again "soap off", the water would again pour down. . . . The only catch was that when "water on" came before "soap on" the water was cold . . . but during the time, "soap on" and "soap off" the water became heated, sometime very much so, much to the dismay of the bathers. . . .

Filthy, greasy mud—the front in France and Flanders was full of it. These soldiers getting coffee in March 1917 scarcely noticed it any longer. DND/LAC

Clearly, there was little room for the modest.

Then came fresh clothing:

> The next move was into a room with a small window where a man looked one over and shouted "outfit". You would explain you were size 40 chest, 36 waist, we had Stanfield two piece underwear. The official would issue underwear and shirt, then you repaired to the dressing room, or "exchange room" where you would shop around, as "Joe" who was tall & skinny would have underwear for "Pete" who was short and stout.

Lovell added that before going on leave, "we received new underclothing, shirt, and uniform, maybe new boots. . . . we had to look smart for we represented 'Canada.'" For their time on leave, moreover, the soldiers could be free of lice and fleas.

✥ ✥ ✥

If the reinforcements tried to fit in with their new mates, and if the men rested, talked, and argued politics, the commanders and their staff were at work. Marshal Ferdinand Foch and Field Marshal Sir Douglas Haig believed that they now had the Germans in serious trouble, and they pressed their armies to move east as quickly as possible with a general offensive extending from the Meuse River to the English Channel. The Germans had moved their divisions into the strong defensive positions of the Hindenburg Line, the best ground in Flanders, and behind the Canal du Nord. It was this latter feature that confronted General Horne's British First Army—and, as was Horne's usual practice, the planning and conduct of the crossing of the Canal du Nord fell to his best troops, the Canadian Corps.

Why were the Canadians used as shock troops? First and most important, because the Corps was an excellent, well-led formation with much punch and a terrific record of success. That mattered. Second, General Currie wanted his Corps to do the big things, to fight and win the critical battles. Canadian nationalism had burgeoned during the war, and Prime Minister Sir Robert Borden and Currie both understood

that a different, stronger Canada was to emerge from the war. Third, the Canadian Corps was at or near full strength, despite the heavy casualties, and reinforcements came forward in a steady stream to keep it so. But the final point, less palatable, is that British casualties in the four years of war had been terrible. Catastrophes like the Somme and Passchendaele had swallowed hundreds of thousands. The politicians in Whitehall inevitably felt the heat, and Field Marshal Sir Douglas Haig at the BEF's General Headquarters came to understand that a repetition of such losses for no discernible strategic purpose would mean his head. Canadian casualties, however, mattered much less to London and hence to Haig. They were a Canadian political problem, not Haig's and not Prime Minister David Lloyd George's—and Ottawa was far away across the Atlantic, unlike London, which was only 150 or so miles away. No one should make too much of this, but it was the unpleasant reality. Thus it was the Canadian Corps that would tackle the Canal du Nord and suffer the casualties in doing so.

The Canal protected the route to Cambrai, a vital German-held road and rail centre and the key to their Hindenburg Line defences, some ten or so miles to the east. The waterway had been under construction in 1914 when the war broke out, and it lay incomplete. The northern section starting from Sains-lès-Marquion was naturally swampy, and the Germans had flooded the ground, creating an impassable morass. To the south was a dry portion of the still-unfinished canal. Inevitably, Currie chose to launch his assault here rather than to try a water crossing under fire.

This was no easy task. The canal bed was some 100 feet wide and had a western bank that varied between 10 and 12 feet in height. The eastern bank was lower so that the attacking Canadians were obliged only to scale a four- to five-foot wall. Behind the Canal du Nord, the enemy had a trench system with many machine guns and extensive wire entanglements. A mile to the east and parallel to the Canal du Nord was the similarly defended Marquion Line and Bourlon Wood, "the key to Cambrai, and the observation post of the whole country," or so Currie described it. The wood was a key Canadian objective. Seven German divisions held the immediate area and four more were in reserve. Crossing the Canal du Nord and taking out the German defences there and in the Marquion Line was not simple; Currie had to funnel 50,000

The Canal du Nord formed a formidable obstacle, as these two photographs show—high banks and deep water. But Currie found a dry, incomplete section and devised a daring plan. CWM/Imperial War Museum

men through the 2,600 yards of the dry portion of the canal and then fan them out over a 15,000-yard front, all the while under fire.

Currie's plan called for the attack to be led by two brigades of the First Division on the left and one of the Fourth Division on the right.

There were three lines marked on the map for this first phase, with the furthest, the Blue Line, lying just beyond Bourlon Wood and the village of Bourlon. The wood itself was to be enveloped by the Fourth Division. The second phase of the attack was exploitation, if possible as far as Cambrai itself and the Canal de la Sensée; this was to be carried out by the Third Division and the British Eleventh Division. The Second Canadian Division would be in reserve.

The enemy knew an attack was coming and complete surprise was impossible. Moreover, concentrating the Canadian Corps in a small area before the attack potentially exposed the men to devastating enemy fire. As Currie wrote, "A concentrated bombardment of this area prior to zero, particularly if gas was employed, was a dreadful possibility which could seriously affect the whole of the operation and possibly cause its total failure." But Currie persisted with the preparations, using every artifice to hide his plan from the Germans. The precise time of attack could be concealed, and the artillery preparation, aimed at cutting wire and blasting trench lines and artillery positions, could also be used to mislead the Germans. There was to be no intense bombardment prior to the assault, but the gun support made available was huge: 22 brigades of field artillery and 9 of heavy artillery as well as a machine-gun barrage. As the maximum effective range of the 18-pounder gun was just under 7,000 yards, the Canadian plan depended on leapfrogging field artillery brigades forward beginning at Zero Hour to support the attack once the troops had crossed the canal bed. Then, to get the guns and supporting tanks over the Canal du Nord, the Canadian Engineers had to do their job of building bridges very quickly. This was a Herculean task—7 infantry bridges and 10 larger bridges for the artillery had to be built during the attack, in addition to mine-clearing and road repairs across the Canal—and Currie expected the engineers to do all this under fire.

Much also depended on suppressing the German artillery. The Corps' sophisticated counter-battery operations had ensured that "the batteries of the counter-battery brigades were moved by sections into their positions . . . where they remained silent until the opening of the barrage," as at Amiens. The counter-battery plotters had located 113 gun positions and, while the artillerymen knew that some of the positions might be empty at Zero Hour, the Royal Air Force was ordered to get information about active gun pits, and did so. Included in the counter-battery fire were huge numbers of gas shells that aimed to make it even more difficult for enemy gunners to man their artillery pieces. After the battle, the counter-battery officer concluded that "apparently the appreciation of the hostile artillery situation had been substantially correct for there were only six batteries active in positions which had not been included in the neutralization scheme." Currie observed in his diary that "the Boche artillery reply was not as heavy as expected, testifying to the efficiency of our counter-battery work."

Currie's was a hugely complicated plan, involving both great risk and manoeuvre, and his superiors had their doubts. Haig and General Horne worried about the possibility of a disaster, and Horne asked General Sir Julian Byng, Currie's friend and now commander of the British Third Army, to see the Canadian. "Old man, do you think you can do it?" Byng asked. "Yes," Currie replied simply. "If anybody can do it, the Canadians can," Byng rejoined, "but if you fail it means home for you."

After a tense and wet night, the artillery fire began at 5:20 a.m. on September 27. "It was some sight to see our barrage," wrote gunner Harold Simpson. "We were on the brow of a hill where we could see guns firing front and rear and . . . also watch the advance." The attackers began moving across the canal at 5:20 a.m. The soldiers of the 10th Brigade quickly broke through the immediate German defence line. The Fourth Division attack ran into heavy fire but pressed on, the 85th Battalion from Nova Scotia getting into Bourlon village and skirting Bourlon Wood. "It was cruel the way they put the Canadians in the assault on Bourbon [*sic*] Wood," wrote William Calder.

It was h[ell] to see those poor boys coming out—what was left of them. I happened to see for myself the 72nd going in & and one of those lads told me they [were] two hundred men over strength. . . . the country is flat with no cover. . . . when they got [to] this gentle rise which goes up to the wood they were simply murdered. Fritz had the wood full of machine guns and whiz-bang artillery. . . . the 72nd came out at six (battle worn) . . . one hundred & four men with the pipe band.

In fact, the 72nd had helped clear Bourlon, but Bourlon Wood, a harder nut to crack, was the task of the 87th, 102nd, and 54th Battalions. The soldiers went through the forest, tree by tree, knocking out the German strongpoints. The casualties were terrible, so much so that battalions had to be combined to press on. But by dusk, Bourlon Wood was in the hands of the Fourth Division. It was not until 8:00 p.m. that the Fourth's assigned portion of the Marquion Line had been cleared but, because the flanking British division had made slow progress, the division could not proceed to the second exploitative phase.

At one point in the 10th Brigade's attack, Captain Banting, the medical officer of the 44th Battalion, watched cavalry gallop to the attack, only to be cut down by enemy fire. The cavalry commander was thrown headlong off his horse by a shell that seemed to explode under them. The horse galloped away, but then returned to its rider. "The horse stood perfectly still," Banting wrote, "while he slowly climbed into the saddle. When he grasped the rein the horse galloped off. I stood and watched him go . . . hurdling shell holes, ditches, and the debris of war." An hour later, a piece of shrapnel hit Banting in the arm, ending his war. He was awarded the Military Cross for "his energy and pluck." That Banting survived proved to be of great benefit to Canada and those suffering from diabetes everywhere.

The First Division moved quickly, aided by two artillery pieces sited on the western bank of the Canal du Nord that fired point-blank at the German positions. It cleared its part of the Marquion Line,

pushing forward almost 10,000 yards to the Douai-Cambrai road and the Marcoing Line. The engineers materially assisted the First's attack. Platoons that had crossed the canal swung around and formed a bridgehead, and the engineers put up footbridges to allow units to get across the canal and reach their forming-up areas. The engineers then turned to preparing crossings for the guns and transport, making use of prefabricated trestle bridges or pontoons. Finally, as Bill Rawling writes, they assembled stronger Inglis bridges for the big guns and trucks, all the while ramping tanks across the dry portion of the canal. "Let me tell you," General Currie wrote, "that those bridges were begun not only under shell fire, but under machine gun fire, and yet nothing could deter the work of our men."

The infantrymen were heavily laden. Each soldier carried a rifle, bayonet, and 220 rounds of ammunition. All had a respirator, a rubberized groundsheet that could be used to create a bivouac, a haversack with iron rations of hardtack, a mess tin and utensils, and some soldiers had

The enemy's resistance was weakening as the Hundred Days went on, but many Germans resisted fiercely and, like this machine-gunner, paid the price. DND/LAC

Currie relied heavily on his engineers to get the troops over obstacles, such as this canal bed. In an era without giant earthmovers, the engineers performed miracles every day. CWM

to lug the grenades, Lewis guns, machine-gun belts, and flares. Every man carried a water bottle and two sandbags, one in four had a shovel, and many had wire cutters too. The load per man was supposed to be 66 pounds, but a bomber or rifle grenadier's load was 78 pounds and a Lewis gunner's was 92 pounds. It was a wonder that men could walk, let alone fight. But fight they did.

Currie wrote in his diary that "the fighting was quite severe" on September 27, but he was amused when he learned that a full German battery of guns had been captured with the prisoners including a count who had commanded a cavalry brigade. "He was very much annoyed because someone . . . took from him his buttons, his shoulder straps, his Iron Cross, his ring, his money, and made him carry a stretcher about six kilometres." Currie gave the count lunch at Corps headquarters "where he paid a great tribute to the attack as carried out this morning, and stated further that in the German Army everyone agreed that the Canadian troops were most to be feared in the Allied armies." Such comments might have earned the count dinner too before he went off to a prisoners' camp.

For its part, the Royal Air Force had its planes in the air very soon after Zero Hour. Its pilots, a very large number of them Canadians, were all young and many were completely inexperienced. One was Warren Hendershot from southwestern Ontario, whose brother had already been killed in a pilot training crash in February 1918. He wrote his parents that he had flown over the Canal du Nord battlefield. "How anything or anyone could live through it, I do not know. I do know though, that all the time I was buzzing around through the air I was thanking my stars that I was not on the ground." Later, he wrote that on one of his first patrols one pilot in his squadron, 19 Squadron, RAF, was shot down, and his own aircraft had almost run out of petrol over "Hunland," but he made it back. "Oh Boy! but this is a great life. It cannot be beaten no matter how hard you try. While you are more or less afraid all the time, yet you are not what you would call 'frightened.' When you see the Huns, all you think about is getting at the devils. You always think you are better than they are." He hoped "I have luck with me and can get a few Huns without them getting me." He did: on October 30, Lieutenant Hendershot's squadron of Sopwith Dolphins, protecting bombers attacking Mons, found themselves up against a large formation of Fokkers, the Germans still putting up numbers of aircraft and still winning most of the air battles with the RAF. Five Dolphins and four bombers went down, but Hendershot claimed one Fokker and drove another down and out of control, while a fellow pilot shot another down in flames. Still, he was shaken: "How [we] got back is a mystery. Everyone feeling done in the rest of the day."

Hendershot's squadron had formed part of the massive RAF air cover over the Canadian Corps when it crossed the Canal du Nord. "I have never in all my life and never again do I expect to see anything to equal this morning's war," he wrote home. "We crossed the line just as the sun was coming up. . . . The whole front was one mass of smoke, dust and flames. . . . The poor boys on the ground certainly deserve great praise." His 19 Squadron shot down three enemy aircraft, though the RAF aircraft were jumped by "sixteen Huns [who] came down on us from above and how they ever missed us I do not know. The macaroni was flying all about but not a scratch did we get." Hendershot survived this encounter and made it through the last few days of the war without injury, beating the

The Royal and French Air Forces had more machines than the Germans, but enemy aircraft were usually better. The new Sopwith Dolphin, introduced to service in early 1918, was thought to be an improvement. DND/LAC

odds: most pilots lasted only ten weeks in action. Hendershot knew this. "You get used to such things here," he wrote of the death of comrades. It was simply "hard luck." After service in Canada in the RCAF during the 1939–45 war, he ended his days as a small-town storekeeper in Harrow, Ontario.

The Royal Air Force had highly developed its ability to attack anti-tank guns and this facilitated the advance of the armour and infantry at the Canal du Nord. One pilot, Captain W.H. Hubbard of Toronto, reported that he had flown as low as 200 feet and "engaged and silenced many anti-tank guns. . . . Countless instances could be recounted of German gunners being chased away from their guns and then prevented from working them until captured by the tanks." Of 16 Mark IV tanks crossing the canal, 15 successfully advanced and only three were put out of action, one by a mine. This was substantial progress in using air, armour, and infantry in combination, a precursor of the blitzkrieg of the Second World War.

The RAF squadrons also continued reporting on enemy guns that remained active. Calls for artillery fire made from the air were answered and many enemy guns silenced by the 7,000 tons of shell fired on October 1 alone. The air observers similarly pointed out troop concentrations and called fire down on them. But the German artillery, not all eliminated by the Canadian counter-battery fire, continued to pound the Canadians, and Gunner Bertie Cox wrote home on October 3 that "the Hun retaliated heavily on our position. Shrapnel was flying past in all directions. . . . One piece hit me on the chest, but it was too far spent to go through. I can assure you it has been no picnic. . . . Constantly on the move. Digging gun pits, digging funk pits, digging holes in the ground to sleep in. Just get them finished, then another move."

For the next few days the hard fighting continued as the Canadian Corps struggled to reach Cambrai and cross the Canal de l'Escaut against strong opposition. Attacks had to be mounted hastily and without time for reconnaissance, and much relied on the initiative of junior officers and NCOs. The Royal Canadian Regiment in the 7th Brigade of the Third Division cleared its assigned section of the Marcoing Line when Lieutenant Milton Gregg singlehandedly found a gap through which he led his platoon. The RCR killed the enemy in the trench, and more men flooded through. A small-town New Brunswick schoolteacher, Gregg

Cambrai was the critical German transport and supply centre in northern France, well protected by troops and fixed defences, including much barbed wire. DND/LAC

The Canal de l'Escaut was yet another barrier to the Canadians advancing on Cambrai, and the enemy blew bridges and destroyed locks. Then, when driven from the city, they left it on fire. DND/LAC

then led the defence against the inevitable enemy counterattacks, being twice wounded, and earned the Victoria Cross to add to his Military Cross and bar. Gregg survived the war and eventually became a cabinet minister in Ottawa.

The 7th Brigade attacked again on September 30, its battalions now very much reduced. The Princess Patricia's Canadian Light Infantry's strength was down to just a little over one company worth of men. The 42nd Battalion had shrunk to six weak rifle platoons cobbled together into two companies, and the fighting that day was especially fierce. The 116th Battalion in the same division had only three consolidated companies each of 90 men after the fighting on the 30th, and the battalion band and buglers were put into the line, apparently for the first time in the 116th's history. The 116th fought again on October 1, and in all 400 of its men were killed, wounded, or missing in only four days. The cost of the Canadian success had been very high, and the casualty numbers continued to mount day by day, numbering more than two thousand on September 28 and another one thousand on October 1 for very little ground gained. Understrength units always suffered more than those at full strength—there was too much ground to cover with too little firepower.

The First Division's 2nd Brigade reported that "enemy machine guns fired at point blank range. A perfect hell of bullets swept about" the advancing infantry "and yet they went against these wire entanglements and calmly commenced to tear a passage through them." Enemy counterattacks were, Currie wrote, "most violent in character, heavily driven home and made in large numbers, with the consequence that little ground was gained." The ground was vital to the enemy, he added, noting that Canadian casualties were very heavy, "particularly in officers, and some of our battalions have none." The Canadian attack had bogged down against the very strong German opposition.

Captain Jack Andrews in the 10th Battalion in this brigade wrote in his diary on October 1 that his unit had moved to the Arras-Cambrai road and then to the Douai-Cambrai road, where it "took over some practice trenches in front of Haynecourt. Batt. was in the village. It wasn't much of a life, no shelter and lots of rain, and no hot meals. We had our cold rations only. While there was a lot of gun fire, the German didn't know our location and we had no casualties." The next day, heavy German fire hit the 10th Battalion, "but we got safely back to Buissy Switch. It was a long walk but we were going out and the longer we walked the safer we felt." As Currie's account, the 2nd Brigade war diaries, and Andrews' personal diary all suggested, the German resistance remained strong, and some soldiers, aware that their comrades had been slaughtered en masse, spoke harshly about further attacks. "In heaven's name," one wrote in his diary, "surely we handful of men (and so few officers left) are not to be put thro' the mill without more reinforcements. We need 400–500 men at once. If such a disorganized mob is sent 'over' now I shall call it a crime." The "butcher's bill" had to be paid in blood; it was particularly high when attacks were hastily planned in late evening for the early morning, as they frequently had to be.

If soldiers had good platoon and company commanders, and many did; and if their battalion had a good fighting record, and a great many

Canadian casualties mounted as the Corps' relentless attacks continued. A dead Canadian lies in front of the wire near Cambrai. CWM

did, then casualties and hard times could be endured. Morale went up and down with the losses, the food, and the weather, but the Canadians now knew that they could beat the Germans, understood that they were on the winning side in the best corps in the British Expeditionary Force, and their spirits were better than they perhaps had any right to be.

Currie himself wrote later about the considerations that weighed on him after the crossing of the Canal du Nord:

> The tremendous exertions and considerable casualties conse-quent upon the four days' almost continuous fighting had made heavy inroads on the freshness and efficiency of all arms, and it was questionable whether an immediate decision could be forced in the face of the heavy concentration of troops which our successful and, from the enemy's standpoint, dangerous advance, had drawn against us. On the other hand, it was known that the enemy had suffered severely, and it was quite possible that matters had reached a stage where he no longer considered

the retention of this position worth the severe losses both in men and morale consequent upon a continuance of the defence. It was therefore decided that the assault would be continued on October 1, the four Divisions in line attacking simultaneously under a heavy barrage. . . .

But the enemy resisted vigorously, and continuing to throw tired, ill-prepared troops against such opposition risked failure. Shane Schreiber called the stalled attacks "the deadly cycle of diminishing returns." The initial attacks would be successful, but when the (often spotty) barrage ended, the enemy machine guns would regain superiority and the infantry advance would stall. Always there was "confusion caused by inconsistent communications and unavoidable delays which resulted in a series of piecemeal attacks." By afternoon, the attackers had to fight off strong enemy counterattacks.

The result was more heavy casualties, especially of officers, and the subsequent arrival of reinforcements, men who knew little. Moreover, the terrain the troops had to fight over was new to them, resulting in units or platoons frequently getting lost. And with poor communications, as the advances outpaced capacity, the artillery barrages were sometimes far from perfect. In addition, because the ground was vital to the Germans, they flooded in reinforcements, whole divisions strong.

In a letter to Prime Minister Borden, Currie was bluntly succinct, describing the battle as "the bitterest fighting we have ever experienced. . . . It was attack and counterattack every day." To a friend, he observed on October 4 that "we have never known the Boche to fight harder. He is like a cornered rat, and I believe will fight most desperately until beaten absolutely and totally." The Canadian Corps had borne the brunt of the fighting in the British First Army. Between September 27 and October 7, the British XXII Corps had 1,926 casualties; the Canadians had seven times that number or 13,620 killed, wounded, and taken prisoner.

Brigadier-General J.A. Clark, a 32-year-old battalion commander newly named as the commander of the 7th Brigade in the Third Division on September 12, wrote years later of his reaction to the fighting for Cambrai. "Never have I felt so depressed as I felt after that battle. It seemed impossible to break the morale and fighting spirit of the German troops.

We felt that this *Boche* could not be beaten," he continued, "certainly not in 1918. He fought magnificently and in a most determined fashion. He discouraged a great many soldiers in the Corps." The enemy was broken but far from beaten, and the battalions in Clark's brigade had been shattered in the fighting in front of Cambrai.

Currie himself put it this way in a 1919 address in Toronto:

> we were counter-attacked by eight German divisions [on October 1], two of which were fresh, do you realize that meant fifty or sixty thousand Germans, all quite willing to die, coming right at us determined to kill everyone if they could get through. And we were determined that we would kill every one of them rather than let them get through. On that day we fired seven thousand tons of ammunition into them. No wonder the ammunition factories of Canada were kept busy. It was fired to kill. If they got close to us and escaped the artillery we tried to shoot them with rifles, kill them with machine guns. If they came on, as they were quite willing to, we were ready to stick the bayonet into them. I want you to understand what war is and you cannot have war without the inevitable price.

At the First Army's insistence, General Currie finally halted his offensive on October 1, giving his weary battalions a few days to bring up reinforcements. His orders were "to maintain and consolidate positions gained by today's fighting and to reorganise in depth." The Canadian Corps had smashed the main enemy defences in front of Cambrai, and in conjunction with the Third Army's advance, they had driven a wedge—12 miles wide by 6 miles deep—into the enemy line, taken 7,000 prisoners and 205 guns, and all but eliminated nine enemy divisions and part of three more. One soldier in the 25th Battalion wrote home that the ground was "simply covered with hundreds of blue-gray uniformed bodies. Some of our units suffered pretty heavily but it was slaughter for the Huns." The Canadian casualties had been terrible, more than 31,000 in the preceding six weeks. Almost a third of the Corps' strength had been killed or wounded, and as the bulk of the casualties were suffered by the men of the 48 infantry battalions, almost three-quarters of the foot soldiers had been put out of action. That the Corps could continue to fight and function was a tribute to its leadership, its resilience, and its almost continuous supply of reinforcements.

The Canadian Corps' operation in crossing the Canal du Nord was the finest example of its professionalism in the Great War. Currie's plan was complicated but innovative, and the infantry, engineers, artillery, and armour had cooperated to make it work—while the supply and transport system, which had to move ammunition dumps across the Canal du Nord under fire, performed miracles to sustain the attack. Neither the amateurs of 1914 or 1915 nor the increasingly skilled veterans of 1916 and 1917 could have executed a crossing of the Canal du Nord. But by September 1918, Currie, his staff, his commanders, and his soldiers had become very professional. As historian Jack English writes, the Corps' "planning, preparation, and execution was thoroughly modern in nature. Involving the use of tanks, indirect fire, tactical air support, chemical munitions, electronic deception, and command, control, and intelligence systems, it also presaged the shape of things to come in the Second World War."

Canadian ingenuity dealt with the conditions as they existed, and roads built of boards were one expedient that let troops, wagons, and cavalry move forward. CWM

Canadian soldiers bragged, along with Bertie Cox, that "it's a recognized fact that the Canadian Corps is the best fighting force in France today." Many more impartial observers agreed. While that might be stretching the truth a little and while some present-day British and Australian historians might disagree, there was absolutely no doubt that the Canadian Corps ranked with the very best British corps and with the Australians. So too did Currie stand high among Allied generals, a commander of courage and skill, a master of the tactics and operational art of 1918.

✛ ✛ ✛

Lieutenant Ivan Maharg, whose 1st Canadian Mounted Rifles had fought in the battle on August 28 that moved the Corps through the outer defences of the Drocourt-Quéant Line, wrote a long letter home on August 31 to say that his unit had received 75 reinforcements on the 30th and 60 more on the 31st, "so we again are all filled up. Also six more officers came in, and one of them to my co[mpan]y so that puts me up a wee step higher as I am no longer the junior sub[altern]...." Maharg's new seniority would not last very long. He would be killed on September 29 in the fighting in front of Cambrai. He was 21 years old.

Although his letter did not mention it, some of the 135 reinforcements Maharg's battalion received were almost certainly conscripts, drafted under the provisions of the Military Service Act, and these conscripts were rushed to the front as quickly as possible. The first conscripts had been inducted in January in Canada and promptly shipped to England for what was intended to be 14 weeks of basic infantry training. By then it was March 1918. The Germans were into their *Kaiserschlacht* offensive and, in the general panic, training was shortened to nine weeks. While thousands rioted on the streets of Quebec City against compulsory service, the war continued and the Allies seemed to be staring defeat in the face. In Ottawa, exemptions from service for farmers were cancelled. Borden's government, its election won, had cracked down.

In England, one general noted ruefully that with only nine weeks of training time, "it is impossible to train Lewis Gunners for elementary anti-aircraft work" or much else that the new soldiers would need to know in the trenches. The first conscripts went to France as reinforcements on

May 10, some 72 going to the 18th Battalion. One of these men, Private Henry Allsop from Woodstock, Ontario, died on June 10 at Neuville-Vitasse. He was likely the first conscript soldier to be killed in action.

Most conscripts proceeded from the Canadian training camps at Bramshott or Witley to the Infantry Base Depot at Étaples in France, where they went through a two-week course that began the task of preparing them for the front. Next it was the Canadian Corps' Reinforcement Camp at Aubin-Saint-Vaast. The CCRC held approximately a hundred reinforcements for each infantry battalion as well as reinforcements for the other arms. Here the men were taught how the Canadian Corps fought and learned something of the requirements of open warfare, and they remained at the CCRC for up to eight weeks. They were then fed forward to the front-line units where substantial numbers fought at Amiens. Despite their training, however, there were some complaints that the conscripts had little idea how to attack machine guns or, in other words, how to use fire and movement tactics.

Hilaire Dennis, one conscript from Windsor, Ontario, allocated to the 18th Battalion in the Second Division, wrote his aunt and uncle on August 23 that he was alive and "lucky to be able to give you some news tonight because I have been through something most awful in the last few days." Private Dennis added that he believed "the prayers of everyone at home" had protected him from "the awful claws of this machine of destruction over here."

A few days later, Dennis' unit fought in the advance to the D-Q Line. His battalion was in the thick of the fight for Chapel Hill on the enemy's main line of resistance. He wrote home that "we had to walk through dead Bodys [sic] all over. And then I was wild. I was right after blood. Uncle it is funny how a man changes when he gets in a scrap like that. We always get a drink of rum before we start anything and then we can go through fire or do anything." On August 28, Dennis was wounded when his battalion was cut to pieces in the attack against a well-defended enemy position on the Fresnes-Rouvroy Line. "I figure myself very lucky to be able to write to you today," he began a letter home from his hospital bed. His battalion had spent a wet night under heavy artillery fire "which was bad enough to drive a man crazy. So after getting the order to go ahead out of the trench we went over the top . . . straight . . . for the

The terrifying power of modern weaponry—the artillery and the tank—are shown dramatically in these drawings by Harold Mowat, a gunner employed by the Canadian War Records Office to paint and sketch. CWM

German Line, and when we got within a thousand yards . . . what an awful reception we got. Fritz open up with his machine gun and it was just like a hail storm forced by a hundred mile an hour wind." Reluctant conscript that he might have been, Private Dennis did his duty. He was wounded in the back and hip in the service of his country and his mates. If we can judge by the relative absence of critical comment in diaries, memoirs, and official records through to the Armistice, so too did the great majority of his conscripted comrades.

Hilaire Dennis was one of the 24,132 conscripts who are believed to have reached France before the Armistice. These men, enough to provide approximately 500 reinforcements for each of the 48 battalions in the Corps, helped keep the ranks of the infantry battalions at or near full strength during the Hundred Days.

It was not only conscripts who made up the reinforcements. A careful analysis by historian Richard Holt of reinforcements received by the 21st Battalion of the Second Canadian Division from January through to November 1918 is most revealing. The unit took in 1,157 men in those 11 months, itself a startling comment on the more than 100 percent wastage (to use a dreadful military term that covers men lost through everything from battle casualties to illness to postings for courses or leave) that a battalion could suffer in heavy fighting. Volunteers numbered 613 of the reinforcements, conscripts 513, or 44.3 percent of the 21st's reinforcements. Most conscripts, men who had an average of 28 weeks of military service, joined the 21st in August and September, months of heavy fighting and high casualties. The majority of the volunteers for the CEF became members of the battalion in March or September. In addition, there were 30 soldiers recruited in the United States by the British Canadian Recruiting Mission, their time in uniform averaging 39 weeks, and one soldier who enlisted in Britain.

The Fifth Canadian Division, kept in England under the command of Major-General Garnet Hughes, also fed men to the front. Currie would not have Hughes in France, as we have seen, resisting enormous political pressure from Prime Minister Borden and others, but he could not be displaced from his post in Britain. The problem was resolved by taking men from the division as one answer to the need for reinforcements; as late as February 1918, the division had 8,180 infantrymen, more than

7,000 of them fully trained. Currie kept the Fifth's artillery brigades together and put them into the line in France. He argued for and won the right to use the Fifth's men to expand his engineer, signals, machine-gun, and transport establishments, and he used the infantry to add one hundred men to each of his front-line battalions as well as 50 men for each battalion's machine-gunners. That left only 2,800 men in the division, and they were quickly swallowed up to replace losses in France. All these men were volunteers. Once they had deployed to France, the Fifth Division was ordered disbanded—Garnet Hughes' remaining influence at home notwithstanding.

Dr. Holt has also assembled personnel data for the entire Canadian Corps. In September 1918, the First Canadian Division had 12,434 infantrymen with their units, 628 in hospital with wounds, 506 hospitalized for illness, 258 on leave, 843 on courses, and 2 absent without leave for an infantry strength of 14,671. The key figure—12,434 infantry with their units—suggested that the 12 battalions in the First Division were effectively at full strength. The infantry reinforcements received that month numbered 1,852 and an additional 1,032 men were taken on strength for a total increase of 2,884. Against this, 581 men were killed in action, 161 died of wounds, and 56 were missing in action, but none were known to have been captured. As well, 1,925 men had been evacuated because of wounds, 99 because of sickness, and 98 for other reasons.

The three other Canadian Expeditionary Force divisions each had over 11,000 infantry, again a clear indication that their battalions were at or very near their full complement. The total strength of the Canadian Corps in September 1918, according to Dr. Holt's chart, was 129,209 men with their units out of a total CEF gross strength of 150,641. In that month, the Corps as a whole had suffered 2,567 officers and men killed in action, of whom 2,240 were infantry (or 87 percent); an additional 831 had died of wounds, with 299 listed as missing in action. The vast majority of these casualties would also have been from the infantry, clearly the most dangerous trade in the Canadian Corps. Reinforcements amounted to 10,751 and another 9,765 men had been taken on strength after spells on courses, leave, or after recovering from wounds or illness. The Corps had lost 6 men to desertion and 15 had become prisoners of war, but an extraordinary total of 11,408 had been struck off strength, a phrase that encompassed all those men who for whatever reason had left the Corps. The wastage, again that dreadful all-encompassing term, amounted to 26,182 or about one in five of the effective strength of the Canadian Corps. Still, the heavy fighting at the end of September and in early October was very costly. The Fourth Division lost 7,352 officers and men in September, and the Second Canadian Division's commander noted that he was then short 3,000 men. The same GOC in November remarked that he had received replacements of 30 officers and 5,000 other ranks since August, but was nonetheless 90 officers and 4,200 men below his authorized strength.

It is also worth noting, as Holt does, that some 35,198 officers and men were serving at war's end outside the Corps. These railway and forestry troops, the cavalry, and medical and other units might have been usefully employed on their very important duties, but they did not necessarily benefit the Canadian Corps directly. The same might be said

The struggle for Bourlon Wood had been fierce, but some blackberries survived, enough that a soldier could fill his helmet in October 1918. DND/LAC

of those Canadian soldiers, directed overseas by Ottawa in compliance with British requests, who served outside France and Flanders and in the Balkans, in Murmansk, and in Siberia. A small nation cannot afford to disperse its limited strength as Canada did. Canadian manpower, hardly unlimited to begin with, would certainly have been more effective if concentrated under command of Currie's Canadian Corps.

God is on the side of the big battalions, or so Napoleon was supposed to have said, and the fact that Currie's units ordinarily were maintained at or near full strength through the hard fighting from August 8 on to November 11 had much to do with their great success. Had the war continued into 1919, as almost all the politicians and generals had expected, all the remaining volunteers and the hundred thousand conscripts Sir Robert Borden had wanted would have reached the front and likely provided the men the Canadian Corps required.

After the shattering of the German defences along the Canal du Nord and the almost simultaneous Allied advances all along the Western Front, the German position was in serious difficulty. Crown Prince Rupprecht, commanding an Army Group, recorded on September 28 that "the troops will no longer stand up to a serious attack." That same day, after learning of the news from the battlefields in France and of the Bulgarian government's request for an armistice, Generals Ludendorff and Hindenburg agreed that Germany must seek a cessation of hostilities at once. They saw the kaiser the next morning and gave him this advice. The events of the next few weeks did nothing to offer any encouragement to the kaiser, his government in Berlin, or his generals and soldiers at the front, and on October 6 the German radio indicated that Berlin was seeking an armistice from President Woodrow Wilson to discuss terms for ending the war. But nothing was certain, and Marshals Foch and Haig had to continue pressing the Allied armies further east.

The Canadian Corps played its part in keeping up the pressure on the enemy. From October 2, the Corps had two divisions in reserve, and two, in addition to a British division, holding the line. Some of the troops were on the receiving end of heavy enemy artillery fire, Wilfred Kerr of the 11th Battery calling the pasting his guns received on October 2 near

Haynecourt the worst "such shelling since Passchendaele." On October 6, orders arrived directing the capture of Cambrai in conjunction with General Byng's Third Army, which was in good positions south of the city. Byng's corps went on the attack on October 8, with Canadian artillery offering support, but the defences largely held. The Canadian attack launched at 1:30 a.m. by the Second Division on the cold, wet, and dark night of October 8–9, moving over the Canal de l'Escaut and aimed at Escadoeuvres, caught the enemy by surprise and in the midst of beginning a withdrawal to newly prepared positions on the Hermann Line. This Line passed west of Tournai, Valenciennes and Le Cateau. Prisoners taken by Canadians in the Escadoeuvres attack indicated that Cambrai itself was to be evacuated.

This was good news, and the advance by the Second and Third Canadian Divisions moved eastward with some rapidity. German demolition parties had blown up bridges where they could. Lieutenant Percy Willmot of the 25th Battalion wrote that he led his platoon up to a bridge over the Canal "and found as expected that the bridge had been blown up. Word was sent back and in a short time the Engineers came up and constructed a temporary foot bridge. My Sergt and I were first across and after getting the men in a defensive position, I started out to reconnoitre. I had not gone far when I saw a number of Huns and these did not give me a chance to fire for they put up their hands." A few minutes later, German artillery fire wounded Willmot and ended his war.

At Pont d'Aire, a more important crossing, a small number of Canadian Engineers rushed the bridge before it could be destroyed and drove off a German attack that aimed to explode the already laid charges. For his gallantry at the bridge, Captain Charles Mitchell won the Victoria Cross, the first to go to a Canadian Engineers officer. The bridge saved, more engineers threw footbridges on cork floats across the canal and men from Willmot's 25th Battalion took Escadoeuvres. Two more battalions began mopping up in the northeast outskirts of Cambrai. The Third Division crossed the canal on badly damaged bridges and entered the city itself. There was some enemy shelling, opposition from a few small German rearguards, but no serious defence.

Cambrai appeared to have been gutted. The Germans might be seeking an armistice, but they were carrying off as loot everything they could manage as they were forced eastwards. Moreover, parts of the city had been deliberately set afire, and it seemed that a serious attempt had been underway to destroy the city. Only the rapid advance by the Canadians had frustrated this plan, and detachments of engineers put out the fires wherever they could. By midday, troops of the Third Division, now under the command of Major-General F.O.W. Loomis, took up positions on the eastern outskirts of Cambrai. The Third Division withdrew into reserve after almost two weeks of continuous action.

Advancing through the ruins of a Cambrai church, Canadian infantry form a striking tableau. The broken chair in the foreground suggests the waste of it all. DND/LAC

Standing as if posed in a central Cambrai square, the buildings around them ruined and on fire, these Canadians had come to hate the enemy that burned or looted everything. DND/LAC

The Germans' repellent destructive ways became the norm as they retreated east. Robert Shortreed wrote home on October 22 that the enemy "has taken everything he could have. . . . He has done his best to stop us by blowing up all the main roads, bridges etc and what he could not take that would be of value to us he has destroyed. Stacks of hay were still smoldering and all the mines . . . were damaged as much as possible." The resentment the Canadians had against the Germans grew the more French civilians they encountered and the more they learned of their ill-treatment, their "life of bondage for four years," as Bertie Cox said. "The Union Jack is flying from every window." Bombardier Harold Simpson was touched by what he called "the untold suffering . . . of homeless refugees, widows and orphans made destitute by the war." And, like many others, he noted the "glorious activity of people liberated from hell on earth. . . . Nearly all the girls and women from about 15 years up are certainly in some condition," Robert Conners, serving in a Railway Battalion, observed in a letter to his aunt. "I can't explain exactly what I mean in a letter but you can surmise what I mean."

Canadians were moved by the plight of French civilians who had suffered under the occupation for four years. This woman, happily chatting to a Canadian, had been imprisoned for two months by the Germans. DND/LAC

The Second Division continued to move northeast along the line of the Canal de l'Escaut, running into significant opposition on October 10. But its part in the battle was almost at an end except for one major attack the next day. The 10th Battalion had an easy time of it, meeting only light opposition as it advanced, unaware that the Germans had retired beyond the Canal de la Sensée. "It was little more than a route march," Captain Jack Andrews noted. "We advanced to the high ground above the canal and took over some trenches that commanded the Canal." But for most of the Second Division, ordered to take ridges that overlooked the Sensée River 6,000 yards from its start line, this turned out to be difficult. Enemy artillery, machine guns, and seven tanks, including four captured British machines, hit the Canadians hard in a series of counterattacks. ("My God," one soldier said as he first saw the approaching armour, "look at them houses moving.") A battery of artillery had to be rushed forward to stop the German tanks by firing over open sights, and the guns of the

2nd Canadian Motor Machine Gun Brigade halted the enemy infantry at a range of only 400 yards. Further Canadian attacks retook some of the ground, but the German line along the Sensée still stood intact. That would be a problem for others, however. At this point, the Second Canadian Division handed over its positions, and General Currie passed his responsibilities, to the British XXII Corps.

The Canadian Corps' part in the battle of Arras and for Cambrai had ended. From August 26 to October 11, the Canadians had advanced 23 miles against the enemy's most formidable defences. They had faced 31 German divisions, some strong, some depleted, but they had smashed them all, capturing almost 16,000 prisoners, 371 guns, and some 2,000 machine guns. The Canadian casualties were again terrible: 1,544 officers and 29,262 other ranks killed, wounded, or missing. Many of the missing would have been killed, others taken prisoner. Colonel G.W.L. Nicholson, the official historian of the Canadian Expeditionary Force, concluded that the "casualties were many, but by First World War standards not excessive in the light of their task."

Parents in Canada, worrying about their sons at the front, were not quite so sanguine. The mother of future Ontario Premier Leslie Frost wrote on October 14 that "these are such awful days although we are on the winning side now. . . . But there are so many casualties it makes one heartsick and sore." Present-day Canadians might also disagree with Nicholson's assessment, but there could be little doubt that the Canadians had played a major role in driving the German government into seeking terms for an armistice. For the next month, the Canadians and their Allies sought to maintain the pressure on the enemy.

The ruination of France was near-total as this blasted terrain near Arras, territory fought over repeatedly, shows. CWM

FIVE

Valenciennes and Mons

The Great War at last entered its final phase. Germany's allies had begun to realize the war was lost and were looking to sue for peace. The German government itself had indicated that it was seeking an armistice, but until the terms were agreed upon—or imposed by the victors—orders to the armies were to continue operations with "all the vigour you consider safe or possible," as the War Office told Field Marshal Haig. The British Expeditionary Force, the French army, and the large American army that was growing in confidence as it gained battle experience were as a result all pressing eastward, driving the enemy before them. The German army was in headlong retreat, though elements continued to fight hard. In this finale of the Hundred Days, the Canadian Corps played its full part.

Currie's soldiers, still part of General Horne's British First Army, were quickly approaching the enemy's Hermann Position II, a defensive line situated behind the Schelde River and in front of Valenciennes. The Corps, in the centre of the First Army, had reached a stretch of flooded ground in front of the Schelde Canal, just to the west of the city, the heart of the enemy defences and the location of key road junctions. This was difficult, boggy terrain, and any assault across it and then over a defended waterway was sure to be difficult and costly. Moreover, Valenciennes, a

city of 36,000, was reportedly crowded with civilians and refugees. The
French government, while not willing to interfere with operations, and
Haig's General Headquarters clearly hoped that heavy bombardment
might be avoided.

The British XXII Corps, also part of Horne's First Army, opened
operations to take the city on October 24, striking from the south
across the Selle and the Écaillon Rivers. Over the next two days, against
sometimes strong opposition, the Tommies reached Mont Houy,
south of Valenciennes. Though only 150 feet high, Houy dominated
the southern approach to the city, and the emplaced Germans, three
divisions strong, drove the British back with a sharp counterattack.
Horne directed XXII Corps to take Houy, and the Fifty-First Division
did, only to be pushed off the hill by strong enemy attacks on October 28
and through the night. The task of taking the feature and pushing into
the southern suburbs of Valenciennes fell to Currie and the Canadians,
beginning on November 1.

Currie's plan used massive firepower, organized by his new commander
of heavy artillery, Brigadier-General Andrew McNaughton, and the
newly appointed Counter-Battery Staff Officer, Lieutenant Colonel Harry
Crerar. It poured the shells of eight field artillery and six heavy artillery
brigades on the small hill as the attack by the 10th Brigade of the Fourth
Division went in on a 2,500-yard front. Five field artillery brigades held
positions south of the Schelde and fired a creeping barrage to support
the attack. Another brigade was sited to add oblique fire and two more
to fire from the flank. Smoke screened the attack to limit enemy gunfire
from the west, and other guns hit known enemy machine-gun nests. The
heavies, situated on the left bank of the Schelde Canal, brought fire onto
the enemy's defended areas and destroyed buildings on and near Mont
Houy that might be hiding machine guns. Howitzers added their high-
angle fire to the explosive mix. Three-and-a-half brigades were employed
on counter-battery work and largely suppressed the German artillery
almost immediately once its batteries began to fire. Crerar's 69 heavy
guns destroyed 110 German pieces and broke up counterattacks.

The plan worked superbly. The heavy weight of gunfire, augmented
by the fire of 72 machine guns—perhaps the war's largest concentration
of explosives and fire mounted to support an attack by a single brigade—

Canadian guns smashed the German position on Mont Houy and the capture of Valenciennes followed quickly. Despite this scene of troops moving into the city over an improvised bridge, the city was largely undamaged. DND/LAC

completely "stupefied" the Germans in the 35th and 214th Divisions. A battery of eight field guns accompanied each attacking battalion and six-inch mortars followed the units as well. The 10th Brigade attack, begun in rain and cold at 5:15 a.m., quickly took Mont Houy and many prisoners, and the Canadians swept into the city suburbs. They claimed 1,800 prisoners, counted 800 German dead, and reported "only" 541 casualties of their own, of which some 60 had been killed in action.

The Canadian troops, reportedly angered by what they had seen of the enemy's treatment of French civilians, apparently killed many Germans who were trying to surrender in large groups. Told that the ground was littered with slaughtered Germans, General Currie wrote in his diary that "I know it was not the intention of our fellows to take many German prisoners as, since they have lived amongst and talked to the French people here, they have become more bitter than ever against the

Boche." Currie was correct about his men's attitudes. One soldier, Harold Simpson, had written his mother that he had been billeted with civilians for the last three weeks "and so I have got to know pretty well from their stories just what their life with the Bosche has been and believe me they have reason to welcome us as their deliverance." Currie's diary note was one of the few high-level admissions that POWs had been murdered by Canadian troops, an appalling breakdown in discipline at every level of the Corps. Today, such slaughters would certainly have created a firestorm in public opinion and a Royal Commission investigation. But after four years of gruelling war, in 1918 those few who knew did not worry very much about the killing of German soldiers.

The Army's official history reported this misdeed, but nonetheless noted that "a tremendous weight of artillery . . . had achieved victory at very low cost." Currie himself wrote in his diary on November 2 that "the operation yesterday was one of the most successful that the Corps has yet performed," a fair enough comment on the effectiveness of artillery to save Canadian lives.

The Fourth Division's 12th Brigade and the Third Division meanwhile had largely surrounded Valenciennes and begun to push patrols into the city centre. Likely German counterattack routes had been determined in advance through aerial photography and other intelligence sources. The counter-battery officer later reported that "great importance was attached to the harassing of all important routes of approach, sunken roads and valleys. . . . [and] proposed assembly areas of the enemy were subjected to timed concentrations from the counter battery artillery." This worked, "the enemy's supplies of ammunition and reinforcements evidently greatly interfered with. The casualties to the enemy's transport were particularly high in the sunken roads. . . . In some cases the road was practically blocked by the destroyed wagons and dead animals."

The city was completely in Canadian and British hands by the evening of November 2, and the attack on Valenciennes became the last major prearranged assault staged by the Canadian Corps. For the next nine days, the Canadians pursued the retreating enemy.

The air war continued. RAF fighters strafed enemy infantry and artillery positions and bombers struck at supply dumps, bridges, and troop concentrations in the rear. In the Sopwith Snipe the air force at last

Two Canadian artillery officers show the German flag they took from above the Hôtel de Ville in Valenciennes as a souvenir. DND/LAC

had a fighter that could match the Germans' Fokker D-VII. The Snipe's capabilities had a powerful demonstration when Major Bill Barker of Dauphin, Manitoba, took off on a solo roving flight on October 27. Barker had 46 German aircraft to his credit and substantial service on the Western Front and in Italy, but his air battle that day, which pitted him against hordes of enemy aircraft, was unique.

Flying over the trenches in a Snipe, Barker spotted a German two-seater reconnaissance aircraft and shot it down. Then he was attacked by a biplane and, wounded in the thigh, dropped down 2,000 feet only to be surrounded by 15 more Fokker D-VIIs. He fired at three, knocking them down, then suffered a wound in his other thigh. Barker fainted briefly, lost more altitude, recovered, engaged more enemy aircraft, and was hit by bullets that shattered his elbow. He fought more of the enemy, his aircraft riddled, and at last escaped westward, crashing into the barbed wire protecting a British observation balloon site. He had shot down four of the enemy. The air battle took place in full view of the soldiers in the

Major William Barker was one of a coterie of Canadian fighter aces. Billy Bishop received more public notice then and since, but Barker was the most decorated Canadian of the war. DND

trenches, and one of those watching was McNaughton, who wrote, "The hoarse shout, or rather the prolonged roar, which greeted the triumph of the British fighter, was never matched . . . on any other occasion." Barker himself said, "By Jove, I was a foolish boy, but anyhow I taught them a lesson." He won the Victoria Cross for this action, but spent substantial time in hospital recovering from his near-fatal wounds and loss of blood.

With his Military Cross and two bars, his Distinguished Service Order with bar, his Victoria Cross, and a host of Allied decorations, 23-year-old Billy Barker was the single most decorated Canadian of the Great War.

The Canadian Corps proved very capable in taking care of its wounded and sick. This was humane, important for the morale of the troops, and militarily essential if soldiers, restored to health, were to be returned to the front.

The system at the front began with the infantry battalions, each of which had a medical officer who operated from and in a dugout near the front line. The M.O., as he was called, was a commissioned officer but one more or less outside the unit chain of command, and a good M.O. was probably essential for the men's morale. He visited the trenches regularly, watched out for disease, treated wounds, and on daily sick parades knew how the malingerers increased their heart rate by swallowing cordite or made the trench sores most men suffered from look worse than they were. Brave M.O.s, like Captain Fred Banting with the 44th Battalion, also risked their lives bringing in casualties.

Surrendered Germans—there were many in the Hundred Days—were pressed into service to carry Canadian wounded—of which there were also many—to the rear. CWM

The field ambulance's dugouts were nearby, and wounded men, if they could not walk, were carried in by the regiment's stretcher bearers who were trained by the medical officer. Wounded men were ordinarily evacuated at night because of enemy gunfire. When a man was a stretcher case, Bert Lovell of the 8th Canadian Field Ambulance recollected,

There were no women at the front, but nurses and volunteer aides cared for wounded in hospitals behind the lines. CWM

the field ambulance squad of four men were called and carried the wounded man to the closest dressing station—which would be in a cellar of a shell torn building. . . . We were unable to carry the wounded in the trenches because of their zig-zag formation, so we had to go above. When the star shells went up, lighting up the area, you froze still. Also at old cross roads you had to be careful, as the enemy liked to shell them. . . . Arriving at the advanced dress station, you handed over your patient to the doctor and staff in charge.

Frequently, men complained that unconscious soldiers arrived with their money and valuables missing, and the widespread charge was that the stretcher bearers from the Field Ambulance were the culprits. The Royal Army Medical Corps, the British equivalent of the Canadian Army Medical Corps, had the initials RAMC, which stood—in soldier parlance—for Rob All My Comrades.

Men always hoped that they had received a "Blighty," usually a gunshot wound to an arm or leg that was not dangerous but one that would see them sent to a hospital in England and away from the trenches for a long period of recuperation. Private John Cushnie wrote home after he was wounded to say that "in a nutshell there is no cause to worry at all because all my 'wound' is, is a hole in the muscle of my left arm. It is about the size of a 10 cent piece and was caused by a small piece of shrapnel. My arm is a little stiff and makes it rather awkward in dressing etc. but otherwise it is fine as it hardly pains at all. In fact as one of the fellows here said mine is the kind of 'Blighty' you dream about." Luckily for him, Cushnie's war was over.

The risk of infection for wounded soldiers lying in muddy water, sometimes together with blood, feces, and body parts, was high, and in an era without antibiotics infection was very difficult for doctors to treat. Still, Charles Savage observed,

Unless a wound was very bad few soldiers worried much about it. What did worry them was just how far "back" the wound would take them. This was a regular lottery. If a big show was on with a great number of casualties coming through, many with quite slight wounds would be rushed straight to England to make room for new casualties. On the other hand quite severe cases would be kept in France if the hospitals were not crowded. Very bad cases, of course, had to stay there for some time anyway. Other things being equal, whether one went to Blighty or not depended largely on how long one had been in France and how easy the examining MO was.

Lovell continued his account by observing that casualties were next moved by motor ambulance to the main dressing station:

> There were three field ambulances for each division, one for each brigade. Here they would receive anti-tetanus shots, wounds would be re-dressed. Name, rank, regiment, type of wound, and record of tetanus shot would be documented by the clerks. All this information was also placed on a tag . . . affixed to his clothing. The field ambulance work was finished. The casualties were removed by other motor ambulances to the casualty clearing station at the railhead, where if needed, operations were performed. . . . [Hospital trains then] could load wounded for the base hospital at Boulogne. . . . Here there were doctors, nurses, chaplains (both religions), and also a cemetery, for the ones who died from wounds.

Wounded soldiers might be shipped to England and further operations or convalescence. Men unfit for further service—the 2,780 men of the Corps who lost arms or legs, for example—could be returned to Canada, although many of the British-born chose to take their discharge in England.

The casualty clearing stations, Lovell continued, were the only locations near the trenches where nurses worked. As the war went on, blood transfusions began to be frequently used, soldiers often commenting on the way colour came back to the face of a wounded comrade who had been close to death before the transfusion. But in an age before blood types had been discovered, there was substantial risk, though most soldiers of northern European origin were of Type O or A and hence able to receive almost all blood. But if a soldier was RH

The treatment available for the wounded was good, with doctors operating from battalion aid posts to dressing stations, casualty clearing stations, and base hospitals. If a big push was underway, as during the Hundred Days, the flood of wounded could overwhelm the treatment available, and men could lie in pain unattended for long periods. CWM

negative, death could result from a transfusion. Still, the risk seemed well worth taking.

Risk was everywhere, Lovell wrote. There was "always danger of shelling or bombs," and, although the CCS were always well marked with a Red Cross, German aircraft repeatedly bombed them, killing nurses, doctors, and patients. Gavin Baird, a Canadian pilot in the Royal Air Force, wrote that his airfield had been attacked by a German aircraft that "went down the road where he repeated the performance on a Casualty Clearing Station. . . . There is, therefore, no question but that the German did shoot at our hospitals. . . . Furthermore, there was no possible reason why he should have mistaken it for something else because their white cross was visible for a much greater height than he was flying as I had flown over it so many times myself." At Étaples, Baird noted correctly, German bombers had attacked the Canadian hospital and killed several nurses and patients.

Some of those patients likely suffered from what was called shell shock. Under the strain of combat, some men collapsed, displaying uncontrollable shaking, crying, or even paralysis. Psychiatry was not high on the army's priorities list, and such men often received the label of cowards, though—depending on the doctor—many received sympathetic treatment and rest. The aim was to return them to duty if at all possible, and rest and sleep sometimes helped. Others, however, made insane by the war, never recovered. Curiously, two future Canadian prime ministers were victims of what was then called neurasthenia or exhaustion of the nervous system. Training in England, John Diefenbaker in the infantry and Lester Pearson, learning to fly, both broke down, presumably from anticipating their fate in and over the trenches.

The RAF's Gavin Baird also observed in one letter that he fell victim to influenza in the summer of 1918, as did thousands of soldiers on both sides of the line—and countless civilians around the world. "I was in hospital for three or four days. Apparently it had been working on me for some time but I had been flying every night just the same. . . . I went over to the medical hut," he said, "and the Sergeant took my temperature, which was around 104, and he said that my bed was the proper place for me." Ordered to hospital the next day, Baird found others from his squadron. "Some of them were quite sick; others just with a temperature. The Doctors did not diagnose our cases as influenza, but as 'P.U.O.,' and when I saw the Doctor I asked him what in the world they meant. He said 'Pains of an Unknown Origin.' I think that was just about as good a diagnosis as they could have made." In fact, P.U.O. meant "pyrexia of unknown origin" and referred to an as-of-yet undiagnosed fever, but the doctor's definition was no less accurate.

Baird was one of the lucky ones. In its more virulent form in the autumn and winter of 1918–19, influenza ravaged the Canadian Corps and soldiers and civilians at home. In the Corps and among Canadian soldiers in Britain, there were 45,906 cases of the flu that left 776 dead; in Canada, there were just under ten thousand cases among military personnel and 427 deaths. Some units had higher rates of infection than others—the 1st Canadian Motor Machine Gun Battalion had 87 of its men admitted to hospital in November 1918 alone. That soldiers who had survived the horrors of the trenches unscathed had then succumbed to the flu or pneumonia appalled everyone.

Among civilians, the worldwide death toll was estimated to be between fifty and one hundred million, at least 50,000 of them in Canada—or about five-sixths of the nation's war dead. Soldiers at the front frequently received distressing letters from home telling them that friends and relatives had died of the flu or the related disease, pneumonia. "It has become so serious," one mother in Toronto wrote to her son overseas, "that theatres & picture shows are closed and churches are only allowed to have one service. The Arlington Hotel is turned into a hospital. . . . You will be sorry to hear Frank Bresetor died of pneumonia last week & last Tuesday Harry Tucker died of it in Ottawa. . . . Harry was buried last Friday. . . . Edie & Nora wouldn't let me go to the funeral in case of infection." What made the flu pandemic even more distressing was that it primarily affected healthy males and females between the ages of 15 and 35. Everyone had been weakened by the war; everyone had been made more susceptible.

✣ ✣ ✣

The Canadian Corps prepared itself for what was expected to be yet another attack. On October 31, the BEF's army commanders had been told that the German was not yet "sufficiently beaten as to cause him to accept an ignominious peace." The chase, in other words, had to continue. Captain Jack Andrews of the First Division's 10th Battalion wrote in his diary on October 30 that "we expected to take part in the next push which was expected to be the breaking of the MONS-MAUBERGE line. The 3rd and 4th Divisions were to go to Mons and then the 1st and 2nd were to be put in when the next stand was made by the Germans." He added that his company had painted their helmets and that there were inspections "coming thick. That was always a sign of a battle."

But there was to be no battle for the Canadians. The Turks gave in on October 30, the Austrians four days later. The offensives on the Western Front were all proceeding well, and the Germans were now in full retreat, including on the Canadian Corps' front. The Canadian advance through northeastern France and into Belgium moved as fast as it could, the speed dependent more on the ground, the continuous cold rain, and the conditions of the roads than on German resistance. Sometimes the Corps' advance was led by cavalry or armoured cars, and if enemy machine-gunners were encountered, they were usually dealt with by mortar fire or Lewis guns. The infantry were close behind, battalions leapfrogging each other as they gave chase. "The hun has been hiking for home so fast," one infantry officer wrote home at the end of October, "that at times it was hard for us to keep up."

It wasn't only the infantry who fell behind. The horse-drawn artillery had trouble keeping pace with the advance, and the lead infantry sometimes outran the supply lorries and wagons bringing up food and ammunition for ever-longer distances over roads the enemy had cratered. Trucks moved at best 6 miles per hour because of the road conditions, and the Germans had done a skillful job in destroying the railways, planting landmines that exploded after six to eight weeks. All this greatly hampered the logistics network and delayed the provisions going forward. When that happened, the men grumbled and complained— no one enjoyed eating hardtack and tinned beef from the soldiers' iron rations, and being short of ammunition obviously mattered. Schreiber quotes the complaints of an anti-aircraft officer who noted that his headquarters "are at present at least 30 miles behind the line & we have to draw our rations from them. . . . Such insanity as drawing rations for 5 sections 30 miles over bad roads when HQ could easily" be nearer. "Too much whisky and fast life is responsible for it all. It is nothing short of criminal." That was too harsh—the Germans had a substantial share in causing the difficulties.

One officer had travelled all day to reach his battalion's rear headquarters and was looking forward to a night's sleep. "But no such luck," John Menzies wrote on October 18:

> Word was received at 7:30 that Fritz was retreating so fast that our front-line people had lost touch with him entirely, and that we would immediately move the rear headquarters up about FIVE miles. It is a tribute to the speed with which arrangements are made, that we were all packed up, all the wagons and limbers and cook-kitchens loaded up and the horses harnessed in half an hour and we were on the way again.

There was only one pontoon bridge across a canal, the enemy having blown up the others, and there were thousands of other troops moving forward. Menzies wrote that "it took us five hours to get to our destination."

He added that their next billets were in a village where all the houses but one had been looted or destroyed by the enemy. "Beautiful furniture smashed, mirrors and dishes broken, mattresses and pictures cut up . . . everything done with a devilish thoroughness only equal to the Hun, and to crown his wickedness and reveal what a real swine he is, he had filthed nearly every room and even the children's cradles. God in His Heaven could never look down on this and allow such devils to prosper."

Others saw systematic looting. One early account of the Hundred Days noted that the German "has taken away with him everything. Not a horse nor a cow, a pig nor a hen, is left in the country. . . . He burned the straw he threshed. Where he could not remove grain he scattered it over the barnyard." Cunningly placed booby traps were left behind. "I heard a story of one dugout," Wilfrid Kerr of the artillery wrote, "in the entrance of which a nail was sticking out inconveniently. One man at length decided to hammer in the nail, and when he did so, an explosion occurred which wrecked the dugout." Lieutenant Charles Savage added,

> The Germans when evacuating trenches, dugouts, and billets, often arranged "traps" for the edification of the next occupants. These traps took the form of buried mines or concealed bombs which were detonated when one opened a door, or stepped on a dugout stair, or tripped over a wire concealed in the grass. Special sections of the Engineers were detailed to inspect all dugouts and houses for traps before anyone was supposed to occupy them. Generally, however, we could not wait and so did our own inspecting.

Occasionally, German aircraft attacked troop concentrations. Cavalry commander Ibbotson Leonard noted on October 31 that "the Hun now pays us nightly visits coming over sometimes three or four times dropping his bombs and sailing back for more. . . . We had 8 or 9 casualties today." Often German troops made a stand, their machine-gun squads resisting fiercely, their fire intensifying. When this occurred the fighting could be as vicious as ever, the enemy sometimes counterattacking in force. The Third Division attacked Vicq, just west of the Belgian border, on November 4 and found itself facing two good German battalions. The 5th Canadian Mounted Rifles attacked across open fields and suffered heavily from machine-gun and artillery fire. But the next day the Germans resumed their retreat, and the Canadians soon were in Belgian territory, the advance speeding up. German machine-gunners would then open fire, forcing the advancing platoons into a time-wasting deployment, but most moved off quickly, their aim to trade space for time. Nonetheless, as historian Shane Schreiber noted, counting the casualties, the German machine-gunners proved to be "the Canadians' nemesis through the last half of the 100 Days."

By November 9, the Germans were fleeing even more quickly. But in front of Mons—a key coal mining centre and the town where the British regulars had first come into contact with the advancing Germans in August 1914, more than four years before—resistance stiffened. Most soldiers had some inkling that the war was drawing to its close, and no one wanted to be one of the war's last casualties, but the orders General Currie received and the instructions he issued were to keep up the pressure on the Germans. He gave orders for the town to be taken on November 9. News of the impending attack produced a strong reaction in some units. One man reportedly exclaimed, "This war's over tomorrow and everybody knows it. What kind of rot is this?" After the battle, another soldier, who lost his brother in it, threatened to shoot Currie if he saw him. Currie later wrote somewhat unthinkingly that "it has never been the spirit of the Canadian Corps to relax in their effort in killing Boshes [sic] . . . . the Canadian Corps . . . would no more have thought of easing up because an armistice might have been signed in three or four days than they would have thought of running from the enemy."

Strong German rearguards, covering the withdrawal of their forces toward Antwerp, initially held off the Canadian advance, and at 10 p.m. Corps headquarters issued orders to complete the capture of Mons the next day. Not until 11 p.m. on November 10 did soldiers from the 42nd Battalion make their way into Mons, followed soon after by men from the Royal Canadian Regiment. Some of the enemy was still there fighting a rearguard action, but at 7 a.m., the town was clear enough of Germans that the 42nd's pipe band was able to parade in to wake up the resident civilians, who responded with "great enthusiasm."

At 6 a.m. on November 11, Currie's headquarters received definitive word that the Armistice that had been rumoured for several days was to come into force at 11 a.m. on November 11, the eleventh hour of the eleventh day of the eleventh month. The official telegram said "Hostilities will cease at 1100 hours 11/11/18. Troops will stand fast on line reached at that hour which will be reported by wire to Army HQ as soon as possible. Defence precautions will be maintained. There will be no intercourse with enemy until receipt of instructions from GHQ. Further instructions follow."

The guns at last fell silent, but not before the final casualties had been sustained in liberating Mons. In the fighting on November 10 and 11, the Third Division lost 9 officers and 107 men; and from November 7 to 11, the Second Division suffered casualties of 22 officers and 343 other ranks.

The Canadian Corps ended the war in Mons, Belgium, exactly at the spot the BEF had first encountered the Germans in August 1914. Currie and his senior officers took the salute at a victory march-past in the Grand Place on November 11. CWM

At Currie's later request for details, official statistics put the casualties on November 11 itself at one dead and 15 wounded.

The last Canadian soldier killed, hit by a single shot through the heart on the outskirts of Mons in the last moments before the Armistice came into effect, was George Price, a 25-year-old private in the 28th Battalion. He was from Port Williams, Nova Scotia, and had been working as a farm labourer on the Prairies when he enlisted in October 1917. His Corps commander would be the subject of much abuse, started by Sam Hughes and his minions, that he had vaingloriously wasted his soldiers' lives by pressing ahead with attacks even as the war was coming to its close. This was simply untrue. For Private Price, the controversy would be meaningless.

Currie himself had written to a friend on October 26 that "peace when it does come must be a peace that will last for many, many years. We do not want to have to do this thing all over again in another fifteen or twenty years. If that is to be the case," he continued, "German military power must now be irretrievably crushed. This is the end we must obtain if we have the will and the guts to see it through." A hard man and not one to trust anything the enemy said, Currie was prepared to fight until the Germans capitulated.

In fact, the soldiers whose efforts had forced the Germans to their knees had known from early October of the Germans' desire for an armistice. But as soldiers' letters and Captain Jack Andrews' diary show, no one quite knew what to believe; few trusted the Allied politicians; and none trusted the Germans. On November 7, Captain Andrews wrote that in the 10th Battalion "we heard rumours of a general peace and that delegates were to be received at midnight. We didn't know what to believe." The next day, he reported that "the camp buzzed with rumours of peace—that peace was refused. We got so we expected nothing, and weren't going to be fooled. We carried on with training." On the 10th, "we were told that hostilities would cease at 11 AM the next day. We still refused to believe it. It was too good to be true." But on November 11, "We held a parade at 11 AM and told the company the war was over. The boys were almost stunned, not a cheer. It was something they had dreamed about but never expected to see. They were going home." Similar words were written that day by Harold Simpson: "It seems we are in a dream from which we are afraid of awakening. War had become for us so real and yet so commonplace that it scarcely seems possible that it can be over."

The scene in Mons was joyous. After four years of occupation, the Belgians brought out their flags and hailed their liberators. CWM

Private Frank Teskey in the Princess Patricia's Canadian Light Infantry (PPCLI) of the Third Division scribbled in his diary on November 11 that "we haven't been shelled this AM so it must be true. Civilians almost crazy with joy. They decorate us with colours & flowers but best of all the young maidens are right there with beaucoup kisses. . . . civilians can't believe it's over. Rid of terror of German rule." And when the PPCLI marched into Mons with bands playing, he noted that "thousands of people lined the streets. Old women cried as we went by. When the band played the Belgian national anthem the civilians went clean bug house— first time they had heard it in 4 years. A man threw his arms around the bandmaster & kissed him." The day after the Armistice, the Third Division's great concert party, The Dumbells, staged *H.M.S. Pinafore* before a packed house of cheering soldiers in Mons.

Corporal Roy Macfie in the 1st Battalion stated that when his unit learned of the war's end "everybody just stood around lookin' at each other. . . . nobody would believe it." The 1st Battalion had had 6,500 men pass through its ranks since its creation in 1914 at Valcartier. It had lost 49 officers and 699 men, and had seen 126 officers and 3,055 men wounded—and Macfie was one of the very few 1914 originals to still be with the battalion in November 1918. No wonder the soldiers couldn't believe the war was over.

Robert Shortreed was on leave in Paris when the Armistice came into effect. "Paris was crazy with joy and streets were impassable. . . . Flags are to be seen everywhere. The French way of showing their joy is to kiss everyone and few people escaped it yesterday. Of course the soldiers came in for their share." Shortreed did not sound at all upset by getting his own kisses. In London, "people went mad—absolutely bugs—Oh gee I never had such a good time in my life," wrote Bill Calder. "Trafalgar Square—Strand & Piccadilly was one big dance hall till about 2 in the morning." From Folkestone, England, where he was training with the Royal Air Force, Bill McLellan told his family that when he went to the theatre, "People were climbing on the stage & everybody was yelling & waving flags." In Toronto and everywhere in Canada, the celebrations too were huge, boys and girls banging pots and pans, building bonfires to burn effigies of Kaiser Bill, and parading through the streets. The exultation was general, though not in Germany.

The soldiers rested, safe at last. The sign pointing to the latrine in a ruined building suggested that order was still maintained among the Canadians. DND

A parade on November 15 featured a pipe band watched by crowds of (puzzled?) civilians.
CWM

In Ottawa, the victory over Germany was hailed by a huge crowd in the centre of the city.
CWM

The return of the Princess Patricia's Canadian Light Infantry to the city in which they had been raised in 1914 aroused mixed emotions. Few of the men on parade had been in the regiment that embarked overseas, so heavy had been the casualties. CWM

The jubilation expressed in Allied capitals and across the Dominion marked the end of the killing, but the pain of the war lived on forever in Canada and every other country that had been involved. Too many men had been lost and too many lives blighted by the carnage overseas. Parents lost their sons, children their fathers, siblings their brothers, and wives their spouses. The dead might have included one who would have found the cure for cancer or written the great Canadian novel or symphony. Many, perhaps most, of the wounded in body and mind lost their chance for a full life in their own country, and far too many died soon after their return to Canada as a result of their wounds. Almost no one was spared the terrible impact of the war.

The overall Canadian toll—the numbers continue to change as new data are found and added—was 68,656 dead, and 176,380 wounded or injured for a total of 245,036. The death roll included 51,748 members of the CEF killed in action, and 7,796 who died of disease or injury. In all, 422,181 men and 2,411 women, almost all nursing sisters, served overseas, some remaining in England for their entire time out of Canada. To get overseas was to have a 58 percent chance of being killed or wounded, and if one considers that only 345,000 made it to France or Flanders, the

No 83 Squadron, B.E.F.
MENU

Xmas Victory Dinner
Officers Mess.
- - - - - - - - - - - -

Oysters
Potage Americaine
Sole Limonde Frit
Porc Roti, avec Saucisse
Feve Francais
Dindon Roti avec Saucisse
Pomme de terre Roti
Pouding d'Amour Noel
a la Cognac
Sardin Tomat et Toste
Dessert
Cafe

- - - - - - - - - - - - - - - - - - - -

Wines Liquers Cigars

Awaiting their turn to return home, unit officers laboured to keep their soldiers under discipline. One way was a lavish Christmas dinner. CWM

percentage of soldiers killed and wounded is substantially higher at 70 percent. To carry this further, since at least eight in ten of all casualties fell on infantrymen, their chances of surviving the war without being killed or wounded were miniscule. Most of those killed died in ways that were "mean, mechanical [and] drab," so Battery Sergeant Major Brooke Claxton wrote years after he had seen too many of his gun crews killed. There was "no heat of battle or any of the storybook stuff—just horribly inhuman."

In the Hundred Days from August 8, 1918, until the Armistice, the Canadian Corps sustained 45,835 killed, wounded, or taken prisoner. This is 18.7 percent, or almost one in five, of the Canadian casualties suffered in the four years and three months of the Great War, a staggering testimony to the fierceness of the fighting the Corps engaged in from Amiens to the Drocourt-Quéant Line, from the Canal du Nord to Cambrai and Valenciennes, and through the pursuit to Mons. The most men who died or were killed on a single day during the Hundred Days were the 960 who fell on September 1; the fewest, 8 Canadians on Sunday, September 22. The total casualties, as always most falling on the foot soldiers, almost equalled the roughly 48,000 men in the 48 battalions of the Corps when they were at full strength. For comparative purposes, the losses in the Hundred Days were also greater than the casualties that the First Canadian Army sustained in Northwest Europe in the 11 months from D-Day, June 6, 1944, to V-E Day, May 8, 1945, during the Second World War.

The last months of the Great War were no walkover, no chasing a beaten enemy out of France and Belgium, and the number of casualties resulting from open warfare was as high or higher than those from trench fighting. The cost of attacking strong German positions was only slightly mitigated, if at all, by the coordinated use of infantry, artillery, tanks, and aircraft. As historian Bill Rawling correctly observes, only the ratio between losses and gains changed. "Perhaps, however, costly victories were better than costly defeats." Much better.

Arthur Currie had no illusions about the horrors of war. In an address to the Empire Club in Toronto on August 29, 1919, he bluntly stated,

> We picture war as a business of banners flying, men smiling, full of animation, guns belching forth, and all that sort of thing.

One, somehow or other, gets the impression that there is a great deal of glory and glamor about the battlefield. I never saw any of it. I want you to understand that war is simply the curse of butchery, and men who have gone through it, who have seen war stripped of all its trappings, are the last men that will want to see another war.

Currie understood what he and his soldiers had been through.

Against the casualties, Currie and Canadians could set the Corps' achievements. General Horne actually told Currie that "the Canadian Corps is perhaps rather apt to take all the credit it can for everything and to consider that the BEF consists of the Canadian Corps and some other troops." There was some truth in that, but Currie was unfazed: "We took care of 25%" of the total German army on the Western Front, all or part of 47 divisions, he exulted in a letter to a friend in December, "leaving it to the American Army, the French Army, the Belgian Army, and the rest of the British Army to look after the balance." Currie, of course, knew of the attacks on him as a butcher, a general willing to sacrifice thousands to glorify his own reputation, and he knew that some

General Currie was never popular with the troops, no matter how competent he was. But he cared for his men, and he bade them farewell when they set out on the way home. CWM

Currie himself went home in 1919, accompanied by his family who had lived in England during the war. Here, he poses aboard a ship with his son. CWM

of his own soldiers shared this opinion. He must have been thinking of the need to make a counter-argument—but, in fact, the Corps' brilliant record required no justification, nor did Currie. He knew that to beat what historian Lieutenant-Colonel Jack English called "a determined first-class enemy on a decisive front called for 'hard pounding,'" and he knew that entailed the loss of life. He was a careful general, one who never did waste lives. Currie was no Haig, not one to squander soldiers for ultimately meaningless territorial objectives.

✠ ✠ ✠

Who were the generals who led the Canadian Corps to victory? We know of Sir Arthur Currie, of course, but his division commanders remain almost unknown today. This is unfortunate. As a British officer wrote in 1939, "The value of a formation no matter what its size, depends on the character and personality of its commander." This was surely true—good leaders can make an army; bad ones can lead it to ruination.

The initial general officer commanding (GOC) the First Canadian Division was a British officer, Lieutenant-General E.A.H. Alderson, selected by the War Office but approved by Canada. Alderson then became the first Canadian Corps Commander in 1915 when the Second Division arrived on the Continent, and Currie became GOC of the First Division while Major-General R.E.W. Turner, who had won a Victoria Cross in South Africa, took command of the Second. When Currie received the Corps command in June 1917, his replacement was Major-General Archibald C. Macdonnell, a popular and competent brigade commander from the Third Division, universally known as "Batty Mac" because of his willingness to expose himself to enemy fire and his colourful language.

One account, quoted by historian Ian McCulloch, remembered Macdonnell as being as

> crazy as a coot in many ways. I saw him actually get wounded one day. He was wearing . . . square-pushing jodphurs [sic] . . . bright white. . . . Somebody said "Be careful, sir, there's a sniper" and he said "Fuck the sniper," climbed up to get a look and the sniper shot him through the shoulder and he went ass over

applecarts into his shellhole from which he emerged. . . . My god, his language. You could hear him for miles around!

Macdonnell went back to get his walking stick and was shot again, the second bullet breaking his left arm. Another officer noted that "there is no doubt that he would have been killed but for the fact the German sniper was so excited shooting at a General that he couldn't aim straight!" Batty Mac was not the only general to come under fire. The first GOC of the Third Canadian Division, Toronto lawyer and Militia officer Major-General Malcolm Mercer, led the Third Division in France from December 1915. He, like Currie and Turner, had been appointed as a brigade commander by Minister Sam Hughes at Valcartier. Mercer died from German artillery fire—one of his brigade commanders, Victor Williams, was simultaneously wounded and taken prisoner—when at the beginning of June 1916, the enemy struck suddenly and with massive force at Mount Sorrel, catching him on an inspection tour of the front-line trenches. He was replaced by Major-General Louis Lipsett, a British officer who was serving in Canada in 1914. Lipsett had commanded a battalion in Currie's 2nd brigade at Ypres with great distinction and then led his own brigade in the First Division. He reluctantly transferred to the British Army in September 1918, an apparent victim of the Corps' Canadianization policy, and was soon killed in action. He was replaced by Frederick O.W. Loomis.

Meanwhile Turner, who went to England as GOC of the Canadian Forces in the British Isles (his title was altered to Chief of the General Staff in 1918), was replaced in November 1916 by the competent gunner Major-General H.E. Burstall. Like Macdonnell, Burstall was a graduate of the Royal Military College and a member of the Permanent Force. The Fourth Canadian Division was commanded from its arrival in France to the war's end by Major-General David Watson, general manager of the Quebec City newspaper *The Chronicle* before the war. A friend of Sam Hughes, Watson was charming but a "hopeless self-promoter" who had had campaigned hard for his GOC position. He was no Napoleon (though his British General Staff Officer Grade 1, Lieutenant-Colonel Edmund Ironside, later became a field marshal and Chief of the Imperial General Staff), and historian Patrick Brennan found "haste and sloppiness" at Watson's headquarters in planning and executing attacks.

Of the seven Canadian divisional commanders, two had led battalions or cavalry regiments, three had led brigades, and one had commanded the divisional artillery at Valcartier in 1914. Five were from the Militia, only two from the Permanent Force. Most were in their forties with substantial experience but very limited staff training and almost no post-secondary education. Almost always, the divisions serving in France provided a cadre of experienced officers for newly arriving formations. The GOCs of the First and Second Divisions, when Alderson took command of the Corps, had been brigade commanders in the First Division; when the Third arrived in France, its GOC, Mercer, had been a First Division brigadier-general; and the Fourth Division GOC, Watson, had also been a Second Division brigade commander. In addition to the division commands, Canadian general officers eventually held the three senior artillery commands and the engineer and machine-gun commands. The latter post, command of the Canadian Motor Machine Gun Brigades, was actually held by a French citizen, Brigadier-General Raymond Brutinel, who had lived in Canada since 1905. His armoured vehicles were thought to be very useful during the Hundred Days (and one of the original "Autocars" is on display at the Canadian War Museum).

There were, Patrick Brennan writes, 41 Canadian general officers (including brigadier-generals) who led in battle and 74 percent were Canadian-born, all but three being anglophones. Almost all were solidly middle class, with pre-war careers in business, the professions, or the military. All rose because of their good combat or administrative records and almost all continued in high rank throughout the war. From the middle of 1916, only six at most of the senior officers in the Corps were replaced for "deficient performance," an extraordinary record. In other words, successful leadership in the field was the key to promotion and tenure, and both Generals Byng and Currie, the two highly successful Canadian Corps GOCs, fought hard against both domestic and military politicians to ensure that this remained the case.

The fine record of the Corps, then, had much to do with the calibre of its senior leaders. As an example, in June 1917, newly-named Corps commander Currie wanted the competent and proven Macdonnell to succeed him as First Division GOC. A senior officer in England, the 69-year-old Major-General Sam Steele, argued for the post to be given instead to his crony Sam Hughes' son Garnet. Steele persuaded Prime Minister Borden to intervene. But Currie refused adamantly to take Garnet, who had not been a successful field commander, and he won the support of Sir George Perley, the Canadian High Commissioner in London. Currie's choice prevailed, Steele was sent packing from Britain to Canada, and Garnet Hughes remained in England as GOC Fifth Canadian Division until the division disbanded in 1918. Such political victories subsequently made Currie's task easier. Competence and merit, in other words, overruled seniority or patronage in the Canadian Corps.

Patrick Brennan has studied the career of Brigadier-General W.A. Griesbach "from untried amateur" to "a seasoned professional" soldier. Born in Qu'Appelle in what is now Saskatchewan in 1878, Griesbach served in South Africa with the 2nd Canadian Mounted Rifles and rose through the Militia before 1914, and at Valcartier he took command of the contingent's cavalry. Soon Sam Hughes assigned him to raise an infantry battalion, the 49th (Edmonton) Regiment, which formed part of the Third Division. He led his battalion from the front through fighting in the Ypres Salient, at Mount Sorrel, and on the Somme, where losses were heavy. "His skill as a trainer," Brennan argued, "his cool head, and his ability to get the most out of his men in combat" led to his promotion to brigadier-general and command of the First Canadian Division's 1st Brigade in February 1917. Griesbach believed that if soldiers experienced success, they would believe in themselves, and he worked to keep up morale which proved difficult indeed in the morass of Passchendaele. Despite the casualties, his brigade remained one of the premier fighting units of the premier Canadian division. Griesbach, like his Corps commander, studied the battlefield, seeking different means to overcome enemy defences. During the Hundred Days, he looked with favour on the tanks, but discounted the effect of cavalry. As Brennan notes, he demonstrated the open-mindedness that overcame military orthodoxy, and his belief in training, training, and more training paid off at the D-Q Line and the crossing of the Canal du Nord. He was, said his division commander, "Batty Mac" Macdonnell, "the quickest officer that I have ever had anything to do with to grasp the tactical advantages or disadvantages of a given situation." Not bad for an amateur.

Many of the professionally trained Canadian military men also had a good war. It is worth noting that the Royal Military College in Kingston produced 53 of 233 commanders and staff officers in the Corps in November 1918, including two of four division GOCs, two of seven artillery generals, four of six engineer generals, and five of 14 artillery brigade commanders. This was a remarkable record for a military college that had graduated only 930 cadets since its establishment in 1876 and an additional 396 from shortened courses during the Great War. It is an especially notable record given Sam Hughes' hatred of professionally trained officers and his role in shaping Canada's army in the first two years of the war.

✣ ✣ ✣

The armistice terms imposed on the Germans by Marshal Foch and the Allies were severe as might have been expected given the destruction unleashed by the Germans on the world. In fact, they amounted to unconditional surrender. The enemy plenipotentiaries had met the marshal in a railway car in the Forest of Compiègne on November 8 and had been given 72 hours to accept the Allies' terms. The Germans tried to negotiate but were rebuffed on every single major item. At 5:05 a.m. on the morning of November 11, they signed, knowing that they had absolutely no choice. The Germans later denied this, but the reality was that their armies had been beaten in the field. If the war had gone on, German soil, thus far untouched except by relatively light bombing raids, would have become the next battlefield.

The armistice terms bound the Germans to evacuate all the territory they had invaded—though, in an almost quaint gesture of military honour, the Allies permitted the soldiers to carry their rifles and the officers their swords. They were to surrender Alsace and Lorraine, which they had annexed after the war with France in 1870–71. Berlin also agreed to repatriate all citizens of Allied nations and all Allied prisoners of war (some 3,500 of whom were Canadian), with no guarantees of immediate reciprocity. The German army and navy had to surrender vast quantities of weapons, including 5,000 artillery pieces and 25,000 machine guns,

Marshal Ferdinand Foch was the architect of the Allied victory, the leader who directed the successful offensives of the Hundred Days.

and all its submarines and such naval vessels as specified. The economic blockade of Germany that had caused great suffering throughout the Reich was to be maintained until the signing of a peace treaty. Finally, Germany agreed to evacuate the left bank of the Rhine and bridgeheads behind it, to be held by Allied occupation forces until the peace terms had been met.

This last clause directly affected the British Expeditionary Force and the Canadian Corps. As part of the BEF, Currie's men were to march through Belgium to Germany and take up occupation duties. The great majority of the soldiers simply wanted to go home as soon as possible, but many wanted to see the enemy they had defeated on his home ground. For most, their return to Canada would not be immediate.

SIX

TO GERMANY AND HOME

The Armistice had provided for Allied occupation of bridgeheads over the Rhine, and initially the entire Canadian Corps was slated for such duties. But the road and railway systems were almost completely destroyed in the battle zones of France and Belgium. Moreover, because it soon was deemed impossible to maintain 800,000 soldiers of the Second and Fourth Armies of the British Expeditionary Force on the march to Germany, the British and Canadian roles were reduced. Now the Third and Fourth Divisions were to remain in Belgium until they could be moved to England and then repatriated to Canada. The First and Second Divisions along with the Corps headquarters and some Corps troops were to proceed to Germany, taking up heavily defended positions at and near Cologne and Bonn. Smaller though the Canadian role was to be, General Currie expressed pleasure at this assignment: "It was a great gratification and honour to us," and Currie clearly believed that the Corps' role in winning the war deserved this recognition.

To reach Germany was no easy march. It was 250 miles and more to the occupation zones for the infantry battalions, depending on where they were when they began their trek to the east. Moreover, the march was conducted in an atmosphere of apprehended war. No one knew what the Germans might do; no one had any reason to trust them. They had retreated in good order, but they remained armed. Moreover, they—or elements of the army—might decide to resume fighting. There was political and economic chaos in Germany, the peace negotiations had yet to begin, and there was anxiety in the highest quarters of the Allied capitals, not least because the Armistice was due to expire on December 17.

There was less concern among the soldiers. For now, no one was shooting at them, and the air was almost celebratory as the march began. Captain Jack Andrews of the 10th Battalion in the First Canadian Division

Under the terms of the Armistice, the defeated German army had to vacate the territory it had occupied. It moved east in good order, only to find a chaotic political situation at home. CWM

continued to write his war diary during the march: "At 8:30 AM on the morning of Nov 13 the Battalion fell in, full marching order . . . and with the band playing and the Batt. service flag carried by a scout, it moved off." The first night was passed at Denain "in large barns and a factory. The floors were stone and very cold." At 8 a.m. on the 14th, the battalion set out for Onnaing, about 30 miles east of Cambrai, passing through Valenciennes—where, Andrews noted, everything was destroyed, the bridges, roads, and railways blown up. At Onnaing, "the Battalion found that the billets were very cold owing to the fact that practically every window in the town was broken . . . [and] that the Battalion blankets did not arrive." The march went on, the troops passing refugees returning home and bringing their chattels in wheelbarrows or buggies drawn by hand, "a captive nation returning to its home." At Hornu, "the battalion had its first good billets . . . and the people treated them like sons." By the 21st, the 10th had marched into Nivelles in Belgium "and it appeared as if every able bodied person in the place" turned out to greet their liberators. "It took half an hour to get Battalion thro the crowd," and the town held a dance that night.

After four more days, marching for seven or eight hours each day, the unit reached Gembloux, passing by roads "lined with war material left by the retiring enemy." But it was raining "and as a result the march seemed much longer and harder than usual." On November 26, the officers went by truck to Brussels for some recreation and did not return until 4:30 AM. The soldiers undoubtedly grumbled about this shameless favouritism,

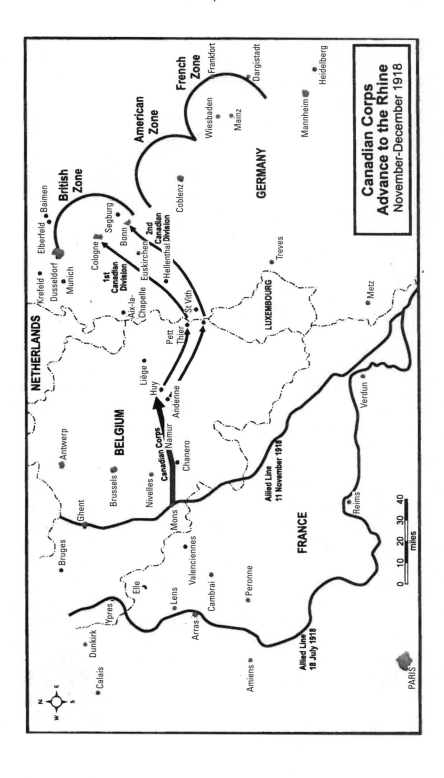

Canadian Corps
Advance to the Rhine
November-December 1918

but the officers nonetheless marched off with their troops at 7 a.m. en route to Petit-Waret. "It was a long hard march 32 kilometres, but the men stood it well." Andrews said nothing of the officers' condition.

The next day at Andenne, "Rations didn't arrive and there were many murmurings against the 'powers that be.'" The reality was that the supply and transport units were hard pressed to get rations and petrol forward because of road conditions and distances. The Corps' logisticians had tried to prepare for the march by giving the divisions extra trucks, detailing soldiers to unload supplies, and moving the railheads as far eastward as possible. But the Germans had destroyed every rail line they could and laid delayed mines in places, hampering reconstruction, so sometimes the system broke down, and the tired, dirty, and hungry marchers suffered the consequences.

"A late start was made" on November 28, "owing to rations arriving late, and as a result the Battalion was still in the Meuse Valley at dark. Marching one mile after dark is worse than 3 by daylight and a very anxious time was spent by the officers." The men became increasingly restive. Guides got lost, blankets failed to arrive, "and this led to further trouble. It was planned to move on the next day but rations didn't arrive, so the troops were given a day's rest." By December 2, Andrews wrote "the men began to report sick with a kind of influenza and many were sent to hospital." The Spanish flu was taking its toll.

In another unit, the 29th Battalion, soldiers refused to march until they received a proper meal. Their commanding officer cancelled the day's trek because of rain—there was none—but when hot stew arrived several hours later, mutinous talk ceased. A similar situation arose in the 16th Battalion and was easily squelched by the CO. "Unit after unit broke into mutiny," gunner Kerr of the 11th Battery wrote, "on pretexts so flimsy as to cause deep and pained surprise to the officers." Resentment against officers was strong. Many of the well-respected junior and company officers had been killed or wounded since August 8, and the new lieutenants had in many cases arrived recently and knew little of war and nothing of their men. Trouble was inevitable—long marches, insufficient food, discipline breaking down. General Currie on occasion worried that conscript soldiers lacked the esprit de corps of the volunteers and might be the cause of the trouble. But Kerr believed it was "dislike of the army system . . . an irritation at the regulations which seemed to lower the self-respect of some and feed the conceit of others, and in particular the salute, the standing at attention, the 'Sir.'"

The challenges for the 10th Battalion on its trek continued—more bad weather, missing blankets, lousy billets. Finally, on December 6, the battalion crossed the German border at Poteau, entering the Rhineland. "General Currie reviewed the Battalion, which owing to continued moving and rain and mud looked anything but smart. The General," Andrews grumbled, "wasn't slow in remarking on this either." The locals "seemed very suspicious and watched every move we made. We returned the compliment." By the 11th, the regiment saw the Rhine for the first time, and on December 13, after a day's rest "to clean up," the 10th "marched thro the streets of Cologne with fixed bayonets. The people seemed very sullen." General Sir Herbert Plumer, commander of the British Second Army, reviewed the battalion as it crossed the bridge over the Rhine in pouring rain. (Another soldier, John Robertson, wrote that "we looked like a bunch of drowned rats.") At last the 10th's agonizing march concluded when, on December 14, it reached Volberg and, after some difficulty, found its billets. "Thus ended the famous march of the 10th Battalion to the Rhine Bridgehead position," Captain Andrews concluded his diary. "22 days actual marching. At no time did

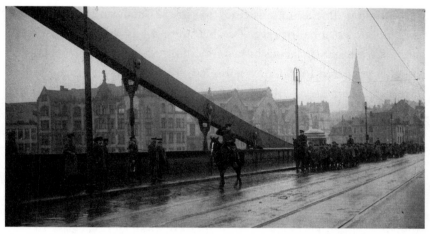

The Canadian units designated for the occupation force marched through Belgium and into Germany. Here, in pouring rain on December 13, 1918, they cross the Rhine at Cologne. DND/LAC

Canadians occupied Bonn in force, the guns of this siege battery soon emplaced to protect the bridgehead. DND/LAC

the civilians show any desire to cause a disturbance. Everything was orderliness itself."

Deployed in depth and prepared to defend their bridgehead, the two Canadian divisions manned an outpost line, a main line of resistance composed of defended localities, and a support line. Each brigade had one battalion on the outpost line, two in the main and support lines, and one in divisional reserve. Two brigades of heavy artillery provided support with three brigades tasked for counter-battery work. In addition to being prepared to defend themselves, the occupiers had the task of governing their areas. The Second British Army declared martial law, and the Canadian Corps assumed direct responsibility for maintaining order in its area, a task eased by a dusk-to-dawn curfew. To the Germans' natural outrage, civilians had to remove their hats in the presence of occupying troops. Nonetheless, civilian institutions continued to function and cooperated closely with the British and Canadian soldiers. Everyone quickly settled into a routine existence. The thoroughly bored soldiers manned checkpoints until they could snag a day pass that let them sample the limited delights of Bonn or Cologne, both continuing to suffer under the stringent Allied economic blockade. There were, however, still enough prostitutes on the streets to infect many soldiers with venereal diseases.

The soldiers' unhappiness continued and increased. On December 14 at Nivelles, Belgium, many soldiers in the Third Canadian Division's 7th Brigade, still angry about the heavy casualties they had suffered in the Cambrai fighting and at their officers' attempt to impose peacetime "chickenshit" discipline, "held meetings, paraded the streets, and declared that they would not wear packs, etc.," in Currie's words. "There was no rioting, no drunkenness, no fighting, and no destruction of property. Everything is normal now, and those who so misbehaved are most bitterly ashamed of themselves." Other units experienced similar unrest in December, protesting against imposed discipline with passive resistance that, if met with force, could have led to much blood being shed.

The troops everywhere were growing increasingly discontented, but the officers laid on lavish regimental Christmas dinners—"It is a long time since I eat as much as I did last night and Xmas day," wrote Private Jim Bennett ungrammatically—sports days, and battalion-run

Senior officers worried about their troops' morale and the rising "Bolshevik" threat some perceived. The answer was training and entertainment, as here at a Second Division concert party in Bonn in January 1919. DND/LAC

educational courses to keep the men occupied. Increasingly, everyone talked of demobilization. Currie noted that his soldiers "are very anxious to get home. . . . We all want to get away" from occupation duties. Private Sidney Hampson wrote his sister that their brother was near Cologne. "It will be some time yet before they go back home, three months anyhow. As for myself," he said in a letter from England on January 6, 1919, "I think it will be sometime around March or April."

In Belgium, meanwhile, the soldiers of the Princess Patricia's Canadian Light Infantry talked of demobilization, but Private Frank Teskey enjoyed his "dandy billet in a private house. . . . Best place since I left home. The lady gives us everything we want—no need to use jackknives & tin cups at our meals!" The two divisions in Germany moved back to Belgium, the First on January 7, the Second on January 19, but did not begin to return home via England until March and April; the two divisions stationed in Belgium moved to England in February and March.

Sporting events were also held to use up the troops' excess energy. A sports day pitted Canadians against American troops on the grounds of Bonn's university, and local children watched the games. The no-fraternization rules had broken down. DND/LAC

There was substantial disagreement between Ottawa and General Currie on just how demobilization should proceed. The Cabinet wanted men returned by categories, Currie by units, and the general eventually prevailed. Combatant units wherever possible would come to Canada intact, while others would be "demobbed" on the "first in, first out" principle, though married soldiers received preferential treatment. Most soldiers wanted to go home with their units. Harold Simpson noted that "I was lucky to get back with the battery again and be going home with the old bunch. There are not a great many of the two hundred and eighty who left Charlottetown . . . going back with us," far too many of them left behind in their graves. Lieutenant-Colonel Harry Crerar, back home a few months before his battery returned, had much the same thought: "I went down to the old Grand Trunk Station at Hamilton, to welcome back my old Battery—the Eleventh. When the regular train pulled in, rather late, on a wet night, about a dozen weary gunners stepped down from a second class carriage. This little party of men was all that returned to Hamilton of this fine Battery which had moved, some two hundred

The First Division's 13th Battalion, the Black Watch from Montreal, left Germany en route home in January 1919. DND/LAC

strong, out to war . . ." Crerar would command the First Canadian Army in the Second World War and try his damnedest to ensure that casualties would not be as high as in 1914–18.

The initial demobilization plan had been to have troops sail from France to Canada, but shipping was short, and soldiers in large numbers wanted to visit England before going home. Currie made the case for this to the War Office and got his way once more. There remained tremendous logistical difficulties to overcome, and the delays and resentments boiled over in major riots on March 4 and 5, 1919, at Kinmel Camp near Liverpool, among other camps. There were 13 riots in all. One soldier, Cuthbert King, wrote his mother that he had been "in the mix up the first night" at Kinmel "but that was enough for me. I didn't see the force of getting my head bashed in by a brick at this stage in the game." Sensibly, he added, "I remained a spectator after that." At Kinmel, five soldiers were killed and 23 were injured in the disturbances. As a result, 78 soldiers faced trial by court-martial and 25 were convicted of mutiny, receiving sentences ranging from 90 days detention to 10 years in jail.

Some units held ceremonial parades. On February 21, 1919, the Princess Patricia's Canadian Light Infantry, housed at Bramshott Camp, England, on their way home held a parade for Princess Patricia, after whom they had been named in August 1914. The princess appeared, escorted by Lieutenant-Colonel Agar Adamson, the only surviving commanding officer of the battalion. All the others had become casualties, as had most of the original officers and men; only 39 of the originals returned to Ottawa the next month. That staggering casualty rate was true for most of the battalions that had been created at Valcartier.

Perhaps spurred by the riots, the transportation of the troops to Canada proceeded much faster than anticipated. The original estimate had been that it would take 18 months, but two-thirds of the men were home within five months and almost all within a year. For most soldiers, getting home was all they wanted. They had sung, "When this bloody war is over,/Oh how happy I will be,/When I get my civvy clothes on,/ No more soldiering for me." At last they were free to resume life.

Private Clarence Elder said after the war that his Third Division battalion had gone to Le Havre in early February and crossed to England. Then the unit "headed home on the Olympic [a large liner used as a troop ship] in late March and got home end of March on 2nd troop train into Calgary, turned in rifle and equipment at Stampede Grounds and mother met me and home on street car in uniform." The civilian soldiers had returned.

What did the soldiers of the Canadian Corps achieve, their battlefield victories aside? Historian Frank Underhill, a veteran of the war, proudly wrote that the Canadian Corps "was the greatest national achievement of the Canadian people since the Dominion came into being . . . the noblest example yet given of the ability of Canadians to . . . accomplish great ends. . . . [and] the visible demonstration that there has grown upon her soil a people not English nor Scottish nor American but Canadian." It was likely so, though the cost of this new nationalism was very high. One point, however, was absolutely clear: the generation that had fought and won the war were, like Harold Simpson, Frank Teskey, Agar Adamson, Frank Underhill, and all their comrades, ordinary men and women. But they fought, lived, and died in times that were far from ordinary, and they performed the extraordinary deeds that made Canada anew.

The Canadian Corps, the very finest army Canada has ever put into the field, passed completely out of existence within a year of the Armistice. Its commander, General Sir Arthur Currie, received a cold welcome in Canada, so completely had Sam Hughes blackened his name, and the Borden government gave him no cash grant, as Lloyd George's government gave many lesser British generals. Currie eventually became principal of McGill University, where he did well. But he had to defend his wartime reputation in a libel suit in 1928 and, while he won against the charges that he had squandered his men's lives, the case likely broke his spirit and health. Only 58 years old, he died in 1933.

Currie's reputation and that of the Corps he commanded today stands very high. The general is almost universally seen by military historians as Canada's greatest soldier, one of the finest leaders of the Great War, a commander of skill and intelligence. The Canadian Corps similarly is hailed as one of the best—and perhaps the very best—fighting formation on the Western Front. And in the Hundred Days, the battles from August 8 to the Armistice, Currie and his Canadians led the Allied armies at Amiens, the Drocourt-Quéant Line, Cambrai, Valenciennes, and Mons in breaking the back of German resistance. The cost to the

While some men tried to forget the war as quickly as possible, others sought again and again to recreate the camaraderie. This 1922 reunion dinner brought old comrades together, and such reunions would continue into the post-Second World War years. CWM

Corps was huge in life and treasure—the Commonwealth War Graves Commission's Canadian cemeteries across northern France and Belgium mark the human toll, and in April 1920 Canada agreed to pay Britain $252,567,942.03 for all the supplies and facilities its overseas army had used—but the Corps' extraordinary victories in the last months of the Great War perhaps justified the price. Currie himself told Prime Minister Sir Robert Borden that, "to my mind, there is no doubt, that no force of similar size played anything like so great a part in bringing the proud enemy to his knees."

The war against Germany had to be resumed two decades later. It was a tragedy that the skills and experience of the great Canadian Corps of 1918 were deliberately tossed away by the government and people of Canada who allowed their superb army to atrophy into a simulacrum of the pre-1914 Militia. But this was no fault of the soldiers who fought the Great War. The Hundred Days was their greatest victory—Canada's greatest victory.

TABLE OF RANKS

Private/Gunner/Sapper/Trooper
Lance Corporal
Corporal
Sergeant
Quartermaster Sergeant
Company/Battery/Squadron Sergeant Major
Regimental Sergeant Major

2nd Lieutenant
Lieutenant
Captain
Major
Lieutenant-Colonel
Colonel
Brigadier-General
Major-General
Lieutenant-General
General
Field Marshal

A 2nd Lieutenant or Lieutenant ordinarily commanded an infantry platoon of up to 50 men.

A Captain was usually a company commander or battalion adjutant.

A Major usually commanded a company of four platoons or 150 or so men or was a battalion second-in-command.

A Lieutenant-Colonel commanded a battalion of some 1,000 men.

A Colonel was usually a senior staff officer.

Brigadier-Generals commanded brigades of four battalions (4,000 men).

Major-Generals commanded divisions of three brigades plus supporting arms and services (approximately 17,500–20,000 men).

Lieutenant-Generals commanded a corps of two or more divisions.

Generals commanded an army of two or more corps.

Field Marshals commanded two or more armies.

APPENDIX 2:

CANADIAN CORPS COMMANDERS, AUGUST 8 TO NOVEMBER 11, 1918

Canadian Corps, General Officer Commanding: Lieutenant-General Sir Arthur Currie

Brigadier-General, General Staff: Brigadier-General N.W. Webber (to Oct 27, 1918); Brigadier-General R.J.F. Hayter
Deputy Adjutant and Quartermaster-General: Brigadier-General G.J. Farmar
General Officer Commanding Royal Artillery: Major-General Sir E.W.B. Morrison
Chief Engineer: Major-General W.B. Lindsay
General Officer Commanding Canadian Machine Gun Corps: Brigadier-General R. Brutinel
General Officer Commanding, Heavy Artillery: Brigadier-General R.H. Massie (to Oct 21, 1918); Brigadier-General A.G.L. McNaughton

FIRST CANADIAN DIVISION: Major-General Sir A.C. Macdonnell
1st Brigade: Brigadier-General W.A. Griesbach
      1st Battalion
      2nd Battalion
      3rd Battalion
      4th Battalion
      1st Trench Mortar Battery

2nd Brigade: Brigadier-General F.O.W. Loomis (to Sep 12, 1918); Brigadier-General R.P. Clark
      5th Battalion
      7th Battalion

8th Battalion
10th Battalion
2nd Trench Mortar Battery

3rd Brigade: Brigadier-General G.S. Tuxford
  13th Battalion
  14th Battalion
  15th Battalion
  16th Battalion
  3rd Trench Mortar Battery

Divisional Artillery: Brigadier-General H.C. Thacker

SECOND CANADIAN DIVISION: Major-General Sir H.E. Burstall
4th Brigade: Brigadier-General R. Rennie (to Sept 11, 1918); Brigadier-General G.E. McCuaig
  18th Battalion
  19th Battalion
  20th Battalion
  21st Battalion
  4th Trench Mortar Battery

5th Brigade: Brigadier-General J.M. Ross (to Aug 9, 1918); Brigadier-General T.L. Tremblay
  22nd Battalion
  24th Battalion
  25th Battalion
  26th Battalion
  5th Trench Mortar Battery

6th Brigade: Brigadier-General A.H. Bell (to Oct 1, 1918); Brigadier-General A. Ross
  27th Battalion
  28th Battalion
  29th Battalion

31st Battalion
6th Trench Mortar Battery

Divisional Artillery: Brigadier-General H.A. Panet

THIRD CANADIAN DIVISION: Major-General L.J. Lipsett (to Sep 12, 1918);
Major-General F.O.W. Loomis
7th Brigade: Brigadier-General H.M. Dyer (to Sep 11, 1918); Brigadier-
General J.A. Clark
    Princess Patricia's Canadian light Infantry
    Royal Canadian Regiment
    42nd Battalion
    49th Battalion
    7th Trench Mortar Battery

8th Brigade: Brigadier-General D.C. Draper
    1st Canadian Mounted Rifles
    2nd Canadian Mounted Rifles
    4th Canadian Mounted Rifles
    5th Canadian Mounted Rifles
    8th Trench Mortar Battery

9th Brigade: Brigadier-General D.M. Ormond
    43rd Battalion
    52nd Battalion
    58th Battalion
    116th Battalion
    9th Trench Mortar Battery

Divisional Artillery: Brigadier-General J.S. Stewart

FOURTH CANADIAN DIVISION: Major-General Sir D. Watson
10th Brigade: Brigadier-General R.J.F. Hayter (to Oct 27, 1918);
Brigadier-General J.M. Ross
    44th Battalion
    46th Battalion

47th Battalion
50th Battalion
10th Trench Mortar Battery

11th Brigade: Brigadier-General V.W. Odlum
54th Battalion
75th Battalion
87th Battalion
102nd Battalion
11th Trench Mortar Battery

12th Brigade: Brigadier-General J.H. MacBrien
38th Battalion
72nd Battalion
78th Battalion
85th Battalion
12th Trench Mortar Battery

Divisional Artillery: Brigadier-General W.B.M. King

Canadian Cavalry Brigade: Brigadier-General R.W. Paterson
(the Cavalry Brigade served outside the Corps)

DIVISION ORGANIZATION

First Canadian Division

1st Brigade, Canadian Field Artillery
    1st Field Battery
    3rd Field Battery
    4th Field Battery
    2nd Howitzer Battery
2nd Brigade, CFA [similar]

First Division Ammunition Column

1st Brigade Canadian Engineers
    1st, 2nd, 3rd Battalions

First Division Signal Company

1st Infantry Brigade
    1st, 2nd, 3rd, 4th Infantry Battalion
    1st Trench Mortar Battery

2nd Infantry Brigade
    5th, 7th, 8th, 10th Infantry Battalion
    2nd Trench Mortar Battery

3rd Infantry Brigade
    13th, 14th, 15th, 16th Infantry Battalion
    3rd Trench Mortar Battery

1st Battalion Canadian Machine Gun Corps

First Divisional Train, Canadian Army Service Corps

Nos. 1, 2, 3 Field Ambulance

First Division Employment Company

This book is based on a substantial range of primary and secondary sources. I have drawn most of the primary sources from the excellent and very large online collections of Great War letters, memoirs, and diaries gathered by the Canadian Letters and Images Project. CLIP is directed by Dr. Stephen Davies of the History Department at Vancouver Island University in Nanaimo, B.C., and it operates on a shoestring budget and with voluntary labour. The collection (which includes material from all Canadian conflicts) is an exceptional resource, and I have made heavy use of the Jack Andrews, Charles Savage, Bertie Cox, Ivan Maharg, Bert Lovell, Clarence Gass, Gavin Baird, Kenneth Foster, Harold Simpson, and other fonds. In almost all cases, the letter or memoir author is indicated in the text. I have also used the Frank Teskey Diary and the Woodman and Ibbotson Leonard Diaries, both of which were lent to me by their owners, and a variety of other primary sources that I have collected over the last 30 years. Most of the unit and formation war diaries are posted on the Library and Archives Canada website, and Veterans Affairs Canada has some fine letters and diaries on its site. A number of private groups, too numerous to list, maintain Great War websites with good documentation. These can readily be found by googling.

No writer on Canada's role in the Great War can fail to rely on the official histories: G.W.L. Nicholson, *Canadian Expeditionary Force 1914–1919* (1962); S.F. Wise, *Canadian Airmen and the First World War* (1980); and Sir Andrew Macphail, *The Medical Services* (1925). I have also used *The Report of the Ministry of the Overseas Military Forces of Canada* (1919). There are also dozens of regimental histories, some skeleton accounts, others richly detailed. Many are available online.

The fundamental scholarly monograph on the Hundred Days is Shane Schreiber's *Shock Army of the British Empire: The Canadian Corps in the Last 100 Days of the Great War* (1997). This is a first-rate study. So too are the many fine books and articles by Tim Cook. His *Shock Troops* (2008), the second of his two volumes on the Canadian Corps in the Great War, is extremely useful, as is his *No Place to Run: The Canadian Corps and Gas Warfare in The First World War* (1999); *The Madman and the Butcher* (2010) on the Hughes-Currie feuding; and *Warlords: Borden, Mackenzie King, and Canada's World Wars* (2012).

A friend for almost 60 years, Desmond Morton is the author of a number of very fine books on military history. His best, in my view, is *When Your Number's Up: The Canadian Soldier in the First World War* (1993), which tells readers precisely how soldiers lived, fought, and died. Morton and I were co-authors of *Marching to Armageddon: Canadians and the Great War 1914–1919* (1989), an illustrated, popular history. My own books that deal with the Great War include (with J.M. Hitsman) *Broken Promises: A History of Conscription in Canada* (1977); *Canada's Army: Waging War and Keeping the Peace* (2002); *Hell's Corner: An Illustrated History of Canada's Great War, 1914–1918* (2004); *How Britain's Weakness Forced Canada Into the Arms of the United States* (1989); (edited with Norman Hillmer) *Battle Lines: Eyewitness Accounts from Canada's Military History* (2004); and (with Dean Oliver) *The Oxford Companion to Canadian Military History* (2011).

There are a host of fine Canadian monographs, only a few of which will be listed here. A.M.J. Hyatt's *General Sir Arthur Currie* (1987) is very sound, as is Stephen Harris' *Canadian Brass: The Making of a Professional Army 1860–1939* (1988). Bill Rawling's *Surviving Trench Warfare: Technology and the Canadian Corps, 1914–1918* (1992) is excellent, as is Kenneth Radley's heavily detailed *We Lead Others Follow: First Canadian Division 1914–1918* (2006). Daniel Dancocks wrote *Sir Arthur Currie: A Biography* (1985), and *Spearhead to Victory: Canada and the Great War* (1987), among his other studies. Currie's suit for libel is carefully examined by jurist Robert Sharpe in *The Last Day, The Last Hour: The Currie Libel Trial* (1988). Andrew Iarocci's *Shoestring Soldiers* (2008) closely studies the First Canadian Division's introduction to battle. Mark Humphries' *The Selected Papers of Sir Arthur Currie* (2008) is extremely useful, as are David Bercuson's *True Patriot: The Life of Brooke Claxton 1898–1960* (1993); Jonathan Vance, *Death So Noble: Memory, Meaning, and the First World War* (1997), *Maple Leaf Empire* (2012), and *Objects of Concern: Canadian Prisoners of War through the Twentieth Century* (1994); and James McWilliams and R. James Steel, *Amiens: Dawn of Victory* (2001). I have also used Paul Dickson's *A Thoroughly Canadian General* (2007) on Harry Crerar's Great War experience and R.H. Roy's *For Most Conspicuous Bravery* (1977) on George Pearkes. Dean Oliver and Laura Brandon, *Canvas of War: Painting the Canadian Experience 1914 to 1945* (2000), has a fine introduction and first-class reproductions of Canada's superb war art, some of which appears here.

I relied on four first-class theses. William Stewart's 1982 University of New Brunswick M.A. thesis, *Attack Doctrine in the Canadian Corps, 1916–1918*, remains unrivalled. Michael Ryan's *Supplying the Materiel Battle: Combined Logistics in the Canadian Corps, 1915–1918* (M.A., Carleton University, 2005); Ian McCulloch's *"The Fighting Seventh": The Evolution and Devolution of Tactical Command and Control in a Canadian Infantry Brigade of the Great War* (M.A., Royal Military College, 1997); and Richard Holt's *Filling the Ranks: Recruiting, Training and Reinforcements In the Canadian Expeditionary Force 1914–1918* (PhD, Western University, 2011) are all fine examples of research that add much to what we know about the Canadian Expeditionary Force and the Canadian Corps' role in the First World War.

Many articles that study the Canadian role in the war can be found in edited collections, including Bernd Horn, *The Canadian Way of War* (2006); Bernd Horn and Stephen Harris, *Warrior Chiefs* (2001); David Mackenzie, *Canada and the First World War* (2005); Andrew Godefroy, *Great War Commands* (2010); B.C. Busch, *Canada and the Great War* (2003); Yves Tremblay, *Canadian Military History Since the 17th Century* (2001); and C.L. Mantle, *The Apathetic and the Defiant: Case Studies of Canadian Mutiny and Disobedience, 1812–1919* (2007).

There is a vast international literature on the Great War dealing with every aspect of the conflict. British and Australian historians tend to downplay the Canadian Corps' role, just as Canadian authors do their best to overemphasize it. Balance lies somewhere in between the critics and the proponents. Among those books I found very useful were R. Prior and T. Wilson, *Command on the Western Front: The Military Career of Sir Henry Rawlinson 1914–1918* (1992); Don Farr, *The Silent General: Horne of the First Army* (2007); Simon Robbins, *The First World War*

Letters of General Lord Horne (2009); John Terraine, *Douglas Haig: The Educated Soldier* (1963); Walter Reid, *Architect of Victory: Douglas Haig* (2006); S. Bidwell and D. Graham, *Fire-power: British Army Weapons and Theories of War, 1904–1945* (1982); Tim Travers, *How the War Was Won* (1992); Gordon Corrigan, *Mud, Blood and Poppycock* (2003); Robin Neillands, *The Great War Generals on the Western Front* (1999); Gary Sheffield, *The Chief: Douglas Haig and the British Army* (2011); Gary Sheffield and John Bourne, eds., *Douglas Haig: War Diaries and Letters 1914–1918* (2005); Gary Sheffield and Peter Gray, eds., *Changing War: The British Army, the Hundred Days Campaign and the Birth of the Royal Air Force, 1918* (2013), especially the fine article on Canadian logistics at Amiens by Rob Thompson; Nick Lloyd, *Hundred Days: The Campaign that Ended World War I* (2014); David Stevenson, *With Our Backs to the Wall: Victory and Defeat in 1918* (2011); and J.P. Harris, *Amiens to the Armistice* (1998).

Finally, there are excellent military history journals. I have made full use of articles in *Canadian Military History, Canadian Military Journal, Canadian Army Journal,* and the *Journal of Military History.* I regret that I do not have space to list the many fine articles in these and other publications.

Although I have not provided any citations in the text, readers interested in further detail on sources may contact me through the publisher.

One note: Canadians during the Great War spoke and thought in yards and feet and measured speed in miles per hour. To translate these measurements into the metric system we use today, to my mind, would distort history, and I have not done so.

Acknowledgements

I have benefited greatly from conversations over many years with colleagues, friends, and former students. Lieutenant-Colonel (ret'd) Dr. Doug Delaney of the Royal Military College generously shared his understanding of the Great War and his excellent articles. Professor Roger Sarty at Wilfrid Laurier University and Dr. Dean Oliver at the Canadian Museum of History know everything about the war (and everything else historical too) and were most helpful with advice. They built the wonderful Canadian War Museum in Ottawa, and CWM's online materials on the Great War were most useful, as were the art and photograph collections of the museum where Jane Naisbitt, Maggie Arbour-Doucette, Dr. Laura Brandon, and Meredith Maclean were kindness and efficiency personified. Dr. Tim Cook of CWM offered useful suggestions. Dr. Richard Holt kindly gave me a copy of his important PhD dissertation on Canadian Great War manpower, and I took full advantage of conversations with and the works written by my former student, Patrick Brennan of the University of Calgary. His are the best studies of Canadian Corps leadership. And I have made full use of the wonderful collections of letters, memoirs, and photographs on the online Canadian Letters and Images Project (www.canadianletters.ca) run by Stephen Davies of the History Department at Vancouver Island University in Nanaimo, B.C. I am honoured to be a member of his board of directors.

My long-time friends David Bercuson of the University of Calgary, Norman Hillmer of Carleton University, and Desmond Morton of McGill University contributed with their work and conversations over many years. The manuscript was read by Drs. Doug Delaney, Norman Hillmer, Michael Bliss, and Linda Grayson, all of whose judgments I value highly, and by readers for Oxford University Press. The editing was ably done by Dr. Jen Rubio at the press.

Dr. Steve Harris of the Directorate of History and Heritage at National Defence Headquarters in Ottawa kindly granted access to his directorate's maps.

Finally, I must remember the Canadian men and women who fought and won the Great War and, most especially, those whose letters, diaries, and memoirs form the heart of this book. Their unvarnished stories, their hopes and fears, their joys and sorrows, are the stuff of Canada's history.

INDEX